Prentice Hall Guides
to Advanced Communication

Guide to
Presentations

Second Edition

Mary Munter
Tuck School of Business
Dartmouth College

Lynn Russell
Professional Development
Company

PEARSON

Prentice
Hall

Upper Saddle River, New Jersey 07458

Library of Congress Cataloging-in-Publication Data

Munter, Mary.
   Guide to presentations / Mary Munter, Lynn Russell. — 2nd ed.
      p. cm. — (Prentice Hall guides to advanced communication)
   Includes bibliographical references and index.
   ISBN 978-0-13-175523-9
   1. Business presentations.   I. Russell, Lynn.   II. Title.
   HF5718.22.M86 2008
   658.4'5—dc22

                                        2007009456

Editor-in-Chief: David Parker
VP/ Editorial Director: Jeff Shelstad
Product Development Manager: Ashley Santora
Assistant Editor: Denise Vaughn
Marketing Manager: Jodi Basset
Managing Editor, Poduction: Renata Butera
Production Editor: Marcela Boos
Permissions Coordinator: Charles Morris
Manufacturing Buyer: Michelle Klein
Design/Composition Manager: Christy Mahon

Cover Art Director: Jayne Conte
Cover Design: Kiwi Design
Composition: Integra Software Services
Full-Service Project Management:
   Bookmasters, Inc.
Printer/Binder: RRD
   Donnelley–Harrisonburg
Typeface: 10/12 Times

PowerPoint® is a registered trademark of Microsoft Corporation in the U.S.A. and other countries. This book is not sponsored or endorsed by or affiliated with the Microsoft Corporation.

Pearson Education LTD.
Pearson Education Singapore, Pte. Ltd
Pearson Education, Canada, Ltd
Pearson Education–Japan

Pearson Education Australia PTY, Limited
Pearson Education North Asia Ltd
Pearson Educación de Mexico, S.A. de C.V.
Pearson Education Malaysia, Pte. Ltd.

10 9 8 7 6 5 4 3 2 1

ISBN-13: 978-0-13-175523-9
ISBN-10:   0-13-175523-4

Table of Contents

PART I
PRESENTATION
STRATEGY

PART II
PRESENTATION
IMPLEMENTATION

CHAPTER 4

STRUCTURE THE CONTENT   52

CHAPTER 5

DESIGN THE VISUALS   76

CHAPTER 6

REFINE YOUR NONVERBAL DELIVERY   110

Introduction

HOW THIS BOOK IS ORGANIZED

The book is divided into two sections: strategy and implementation.

Part 1: Presentation Strategy (Chapters 1–3)

Effective presentations are based on effective presentation strategy. Effective strategy, in turn, is based on three strategic variables: audience, intent, and message. Together, they form what we refer to as "AIM" strategy.

- *Chapter 1: Analyze the Audience.* This chapter explains how to answer the questions: (1) Who are they? (2) What do they know and expect? (3) What do they feel? and (4) What will persuade them?
- *Chapter 2: Identify Your Intent.* This chapter recommends that you (1) consider your general purpose, (2) write a presentation objective, and (3) use this objective to keep you focused as you prepare and present.
- *Chapter 3: Make the Most of the Message.* This chapter shares techniques to help you make your message memorable and explains why you need to confirm that a presentation is the right medium for your message.

Part II: Presentation Implementation (Chapters 4–6)

Successful presentations apply the AIM strategy to the three implementation components discussed in the second part of this book: structure the content, design the visuals, and refine your nonverbal delivery.

- *Chapter 4: Structure the Content.* This chapter takes you through the process of structuring your presentation: (1) collecting, focusing, and ordering information; (2) deciding what to say in the opening, body, and closing of your talk; and (3) preparing for the audience's questions.

- *Chapter 5: Designing Visual Aids.* After reviewing various visual aid options, this chapter shares five guidelines for designing effective visuals: (1) decide on the type of visual, (2) begin with your message titles, (3) "think visually" as you design, (4) use readable and simple layouts, and (5) ensure consistent and correct results.

- *Chapter 6: Refine Your Nonverbal Delivery.* The final aspect of preparing your presentation involves your nonverbal skills—how you look and sound to your audience. This chapter explains how to (1) analyze your nonverbal style, (2) practice your delivery, (3) manage your nervous symptoms.

ACKNOWLEDGMENTS

Thanks to the many people who helped us with the second edition of this book including our brilliant and speedy reviewers: Lynn Hamilton, McIntire School, University of Virginia; Neal Hartman and JoAnne Yates, Sloan School, MIT; Irv Schenkler, Stern School, New York University; and Josiah Starling, Fuqua School, Duke University.

MM: I am grateful to the thousands of executives and students I've been privileged to teach; to my colleagues at MCA and ABC; to my friends Karla and Claire for listening; and, most of all, to my friend and coauthor Lynn Russell for putting up with me and always striving for excellence.

LR: Thanks to my coauthor and friend Mary Munter whose work has impressed me from the moment I read it; to Irv Schenkler who reviewed the manuscript several times and made many important additions; to Jane Seskin, a great writer and advisor; and to Joann Baney, my business partner and a supportive friend. In addition, I want to express appreciation for my family because the time spent working on this book was time not available for them: to my husband because he is just plain wonderful; to my dad, Bill Russell, a guy with golden tonsils and a silver tongue, who taught me more about selling than I ever learned from a book; to my generous mom, Amy, who was my first editor and who will always be my most supportive reader; to Nettie, a loving mama and an amazing hero; and in memory of Wolf, who was truly an angel.

Finally, we would like to acknowledge our sources listed in the bibliography.

Mary Munter
Tuck School of Business
Dartmouth College

Lynn Russell
Professional Development Company

PART I

Strategy Framework

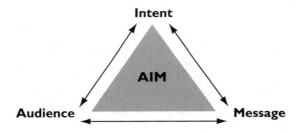

PART I

Presentation Strategy

Many people dislike the idea of giving a presentation. Some immediately start to worry about how they'll look or sound. Others become obsessed with making great visual aids. And others simply procrastinate, figuring they'll just "wing it" or recycle a presentation they've given before. Not one of these choices guards against a major presentation misfire. Nor do they consider the single most important factor in determining the success of your presentation. That factor is presentation strategy.

Applying strategy is the secret to presentation success. Unfortunately, many presenters don't think strategically. They shoot themselves in the foot, so to speak, because they "fire" before they "aim." Many give little thought to their audience, rely on vague or unstated goals, and deliver in-the-moment messages that may not even be suited to a presentation. To avoid this syndrome, consider audience, intent, and message strategy, which we have summed up as AIM:

- **A** = Analyze the Audience (Chapter 1)
- **I** = Identify Your Intent (Chapter 2)
- **M** = Make the Most of the Message (Chapter 3)

As you can see on the diagram to the left, the three AIM components interact. As a result, you won't be thinking about audience, intent, and message in lockstep order; instead, you will discover that each AIM element influences the others. For example, what you intend to accomplish will be based on what you know about your audience. Similarly, which messages you decide to highlight will be linked to what you've identified as your intent.

You may be tempted to begin by thinking about what you'll say, what slides you'll use, or how you'll look and sound, but be patient; each of these implementation concerns is covered in Part II. Instead, start with strategy: avoid a presentation misfire by taking the time to AIM.

3

CHAPTER I OUTLINE

I. WHO ARE THEY?
   1. Start with the primary audience.
   2. Identify the people with influence.
   3. Remember the secondary audiences.

II. WHAT DO THEY KNOW AND EXPECT?
   1. Consider what they know.
   2. Check their expectations.

III. WHAT DO THEY FEEL?
   1. Empathize with their emotions and interest level.
   2. Determine their probable bias.

IV. WHAT WILL PERSUADE THEM?
   1. Appeals that address their objections
   2. Benefit statements that build support
   3. Credibility tips that focus on you

CHAPTER I

Analyze the Audience

Analyzing the audience is an essential part of presentation strategy. A good analysis requires going beyond your initial assumptions. It involves gathering information about the people who will be listening to and be affected by your talk.

As you analyze the audience, try to do more than just reflect on your past speaking experiences. If done well, your analysis will involve picking up the phone, sending emails, meeting with people who will be in the audience, or talking to someone who is familiar with the group. It will also involve empathizing with the audience—imagining what it's like to walk in their shoes.

Much of what you need to know about your audience can be learned by getting detailed answers to the four questions covered in this chapter: (1) Who are they? (2) What do they know and expect? (3) What do they feel? (4) What will persuade them?

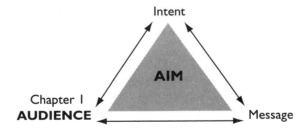

1. WHO ARE THEY?

The first question encourages you to acquire general information about your audience—including demographic data about the group, and facts and anecdotes about individuals. Start with the primary audience, which includes everyone who will be in the room listening to your talk, especially those who have the most influence. And remember the secondary or hidden audiences: they are the people who will hear about your presentation or be affected by it, even if they won't be in the room on the day you present.

1. Start with the primary audience.

The complexity of analyzing your primary audience depends on several variables: the size of the group, their location, the time you have for your analysis, and, perhaps most significantly, your relationship with the group. For instance, it's fairly easy to gather information about six colleagues who work in your office. On the other hand, when the audience is hundreds of strangers, you'll need more time and effort to get answers to your questions.

When the audience is unknown, begin by locating the people who can help you with your analysis. Next, collect group data and unearth details about individuals. Then, try to keep adding and assimilating information up to and including the day of your talk.

- *Get inside information.* When you are an outsider—whether you're from a different country or just a different department—you need to talk to someone who is part of the group. Ideally, use more than one source. If one of these people seems especially helpful and credible, then request a follow-up conversation so you'll have help clarifying vague information or deciphering conflicting views.
- *Collect demographic data.* Find out how many people will be attending your presentation. Inquire about the audience's age range and level of education. Ask about the nature of their jobs. Gather all the data you can, including information about gender, religion, race, and culture.
- *Learn about group preferences and tendencies.* Pose questions to get a better idea about who they are. For instance, ask what they like in terms of delivery style, whether they have different levels of fluency with the language you will be using, if they tend to be talkative, punctual, informal, and so on.

- *Inquire about individuals.* If you can, learn where they work, for whom they work, what they studied, and where they went to school. Ask how well they know others in the audience and find out who knows the most about your topic. Also determine whether you can already identify the people with influence.

- *Continue collecting information.* Audience analysis doesn't end as soon as you've put together your notes. You can keep gathering information about the audience even on the day you present. Meet the people who arrive early, watch for reactions to what you say, and listen carefully to the questions people ask.

When the audience is familiar, you will need less help; however, just because you already know many, most, or all the audience members doesn't mean you can skip audience analysis. It simply means the process will be easier, and you'll have more time for the difficult parts of your analysis.

Begin by confirming the demographic data and thinking about the group's traits. However, don't rely on your assumptions alone. When considering the audience's preferences, tendencies, and opinions, discuss your perceptions with others and use tools, like assessment instruments or opinion surveys, to get an even better understanding of who they are.

- *Confirm demographic data.* If you know the group well, you can figure out most of the demographic data on your own. Nevertheless, gauge the audience's size either by requesting that people confirm their attendance or by asking the person who's handling logistics about the group's maximum and minimum size.

- *Analyze group preferences and tendencies.* Think about what the audience likes and dislikes and how they typically behave. Do they engage in small talk and enjoy humor or do they tend to be all business? Do they like to challenge ideas or do they need to be encouraged to voice their doubts? Will they ask for details or do they dread minutia? Also consider the difference between behavior and preference. Just because many people in a group routinely behave in one way, it doesn't mean that all members of the group have a preference for this behavior.

- *Use assessment tools.* If your work group has gone through a training program that used assessment tools—such as the Myers-Briggs Type Indicator (MBTI) or TRACOM's Social Styles—keep in mind what you know about people's preferences and styles, especially if you know this information about one of the decision makers.

- *Consider using an opinion survey.* If you want to learn about their opinions, ask them to fill out a brief questionnaire. Make it anonymous if you're the boss and you want a true assessment of their opinions rather than their best guess about what you want to hear. If the group is large, you can contact a small, random sample to get a general idea about the group's views.

2. Identify the people with influence.

Typically, there will be more than one influential audience member. Sometimes these people will be sitting in the room. In other situations, they will only hear about your presentation from someone else. If you're fortunate, you will already know who they are; in other cases, you'll need to identify them before you can analyze what appeals to them.

Focus on three important roles.   Identify the decision makers, opinion leaders, and gatekeepers, especially if you are giving a sales presentation.

- *Decision makers have direct power or influence.* A decision maker may by easy to spot because she's your boss, potential boss, client, or customer; however, titles alone may not be enough to identify the decision makers. For example, in some cases, decision making may be a group effort, and you will want to determine exactly who's on the decision-making team.

- *Opinion leaders shape views indirectly.* Unlike decision makers, opinion leaders don't have the authority to approve your request. What they do have is lots of credibility with the audience and the ability to shape the audience's perception of you and your ideas. Opinion leaders tend to be hard to identify if you are not familiar with the audience. Nevertheless, if you know who they are, keep in mind how and when they might use their influence.

- *Gatekeepers control the flow of information.* If the decision makers are not in the room, you will need to route your message through someone else, known as the gatekeeper. This person has direct access to the people you need to reach. Learn all you can about the gatekeeper to decrease the chances of your message being blocked, misrepresented, or misunderstood.

Consider their preferences. If you know little about these audience members, then ask others about them and think about what would influence you if you were in one of these roles. Analyzing decision makers, opinion leaders, and gatekeepers is certainly easier if you've presented to them before. In such cases, think about which of your appeals seemed to impress them and which ones they tended to ignore.

Also recall what they've said about their preferences and analyze the types of appeals they tend to use. Sometimes, people employ persuasive techniques that they themselves find compelling. For instance, if your boss frequently wants to find out what your competitors are doing, he might be a fan of benchmarking. Yet other people like to see themselves or their organizations as leaders and not followers. As a result, they might have little interest in benchmarking data, preferring to blaze new trails rather than follow "best practices." You'll find more information about benchmarking and other types of persuasive appeals on pages 17–23.

3. Remember secondary audiences.

Because they are hidden, secondary audiences are often overlooked. They shouldn't be. These frequently forgotten audience members can influence the effectiveness of your presentation. Therefore, ask yourself: (1) "Who else may hear or see the messages intended for my primary audience?" and (2) "Who else may be interested in or affected by my talk?"

Considering the secondary audience will benefit you in several ways. Your awareness may enable you to reach a decision maker not in the room, send an important message to a wider audience, build support for your ideas, or enhance your reputation as an advocate or expert. This awareness can also give you more control over who hears confidential information. So, at the very least, analyzing the secondary audience should enable you to gain allies or limit leaks.

Gaining allies: Often, presentations have a ripple effect. You deliver your message to the primary audience and they, in turn, share this information with others. To take advantage of this process . . .

- *Ask audience members* to pass along your important messages so others can hear your ideas and understand your views.
- *Create clear handouts* that will make your points for you; encourage people in the room to take and distribute your materials.
- *Reach out to those who will be affected by your recommendations*, such as the people who will end up doing the work. They will be more likely to follow your suggestions if you provide detailed instructions and find a way to emphasize the value of what they're being asked to do.

Limiting leaks: If you plan to present confidential information, recognize the danger of including this information in hard or electronic copy. It's exceptionally difficult to control who will see your printed or emailed materials. Even if you only share your confidential remarks with the group, you may still have trouble controlling who hears them. One-on-one conversations are better than group venues if your goal is to ensure confidentiality.

II. WHAT DO THEY KNOW AND EXPECT?

Long before you decide what you plan to say, you'll want to find out (1) what they know about you and your topic, and (2) what they expect in terms of format.

1. Consider what they know.

Think about not only the audience's educational background and work experience, but also about the topic, the language, and your credibility.

Empathize with the beginners.   Determine what will be new or confusing.

- *Identify the jargon.* All groups have lingo that is commonly understood within the group. Jargon can become so commonplace that people forget they're using it. For instance, a word as simple as "bus" will mean something very different to an emergency medical technician than it will to a commuter.

- *Simplify the information.* Focus on the ideas that are essential instead of those that aren't needed to grasp the main point. Use familiar examples to explain difficult concepts. Try comparing a complex procedure to an everyday activity or incorporating several concrete examples to make an abstract idea less confusing.

Deal with mixed background needs.   Some of these tips may be helpful if your audience includes both experts and novices.

- *Open with an informal poll.* At the start of your talk, ask audience members about their level of expertise. Experts may be more willing to listen to background information once they learn that others don't share their expertise.

- *Provide background material.* Send the beginners an article or CD that provides an overview of the topic or add a glossary of technical terms to your handouts.

- *Invite the experts to be part of the talk.* Before the talk, include experts by asking their opinion about how to make the material appropriate for others. During your talk, ask them to elaborate on one of your points, discuss recent examples, or respond to questions related to their special knowledge.

Address second language issues. Here are some techniques you can use to help the non-native speakers in your audience.

- *Check your use of idioms and metaphors.* Common expressions may seem perplexing to someone who's new to a language. So rather than reminding people to "dot their i's and cross their t's," consider asking them to "check the details." Similarly, sports metaphors cause confusion if your listeners aren't familiar with the sport, which means they may not know that a "slam dunk" is a sure thing.

- *Avoid sarcasm and be careful with humor.* Sarcasm depends on vocal tone; it often does not make sense to someone from another culture. Similarly, humor based on puns or culturally-based information may not be understood.

- *Adjust your delivery.* Enunciate clearly and speak a little slower, especially at the beginning. Use visual aids so people can both see and hear your important points.

Determine what the audience knows about you. Credibility refers to the audience's opinion of you—how they perceive your competence and character. Each audience member will have his or her own ideas about what makes you credible, which means your credibility will vary from one audience member to another and from one situation to the next. Credibility is difficult to assess because even people who know you well will probably be startled if you ask them for an assessment of your competence or character. As a result, you will often be forced to rely on assumptions. As discussed on pages 22–23, your credibility will often change as a result of your presentation. Nevertheless, you may want to begin thinking about credibility by considering these questions:

- Have they met me before?
- If not, what sort of first impression will they form?
- What have they read or heard about me?
- What do they know about my education and experience?
- Will they view me as an expert on this topic?
- In what ways will they consider me to be similar to them?
- Do they think that I'll be advocating for a cause or position?
- Will they view me more favorably if I discuss conflicting views?

2. Check their expectations.

If you are presenting to people in your department, you are likely to be aware of the group's expectations about format. However, when you are presenting to people in a different culture, each and every aspect of your presentation will be influenced by the cultural context in which you are communicating. Our definition of "culture" includes factors as wide-ranging as country, region, industry, organization, gender, ethnic group, and work group. The material in this book focuses on giving presentations in a so-called "Western business culture." If you are presenting in another culture, think about how these guidelines need to be adapted to their cultural expectations.

Format expectations: Format refers to everything from logistical considerations to communication norms. Ask what's expected in terms of timing, visual aid use, formality, and the ground rules for handling question and answer sessions (Q&A). Sometimes, groups will be flexible, caring little if you do something unexpected. In other cases, failing to meet their expectations can cause problems. Don't risk irritating the people you're hoping to influence; if you plan to go against the norm, be prepared to explain why you are engaging in the unexpected.

- *Timing:* Ask how long your presentation should be, where it fits on the agenda, and when breaks occur. You don't want to waste time preparing a one-hour presentation if your audience expects a 15-minute talk.

- *Visual aids:* Find out what's expected and what's possible. You may decide to go with the norm and use PowerPoint like everyone else on the agenda, or you may discover that the group has grown weary of slide presentations and prefers that you do something else.

- *Formality:* Ask how to address members of the audience, what's appropriate in terms of dress, and whether to use an informal or formal delivery style. You don't want to discover, after the talk, that Martha preferred to be called Dr. Stodt or that your interpretation of "business casual" violated the company's dress code.

- *Q&A:* Inquire whether you should expect questions throughout your talk or at the end. Find out how much time to allot for discussion. If the group has a history of posing challenging questions, learn about this tendency so you can prepare.

Cultural expectations: If you are planning to present in a new country, to international visitors, in a different part of the country, or to any group in which you are an outsider, then get assistance from someone who knows that culture. Reynolds and Valentine's *Guide to Cross-Cultural Communication*, another book in this series cited on page 137, covers many relevant issues, including some of the following cultural differences:

- *Perception of time:* Some cultures view sticking to the agenda as a necessity; others have a more limited use for schedules. In addition, some cultures place great value on the past, others concentrate on the present, and still others focus on the future.

- *Differences in motivation:* Some cultures value material wealth and acquisition; others place greater value on relationships, status, or personal growth. Don't assume that your audience is motivated by the same factors that influence you.

- *Factors influencing your credibility:* Some cultures prize wisdom, age, and experience, while others seem more impressed with innovation, youth, and risk taking. Some readily accept women as experts and decision makers, while others tend to have difficulty seeing women in such roles.

- *Expectations about delivery:* Cultural norms determine if you're speaking too quickly or slowly, too loudly or softly, or too much or too little. They can even change the meaning of your gestures.

- *Reactions to colors:* Different groups have different associations with colors. For example, some business people may associate red with bad financial news. On the other hand, in places like Beijing, red would likely be considered a joyful color with many positive associations; nevertheless, to write a person's name in red might link that name to death—demonstrating that reactions to color are both varied and complex.

- *Expectations about space:* Cultures have different norms about how to use space effectively. You might be viewed as "distant" if you maintain too much space between you and your listeners or you might make others uncomfortable if you get too close and violate their personal space. Termed "the hidden dimension" by author Edward Hall, these space boundaries vary by culture.

- *Norms about the communication medium:* Some cultures routinely use email, while others encourage face-to-face hallway discussions. In some organizations, formal presentations are common, while in others they are rare. If you are new to an organization, ask about these norms.

III. WHAT DO THEY FEEL?

Business audiences are not driven by facts and rationality alone. Therefore, you need to analyze the group's emotions, interest level, and bias.

1. Empathize with their emotions and interest level.

Try to put yourself in your audience's shoes to figure out their emotions and interest level.

Gauge their emotions. They may have a range of feelings about you and your message. Some of their emotions may be positive. For instance, perhaps your mentor is in the audience feeling pride and enjoyment. On the other hand, perhaps a rival is also there, experiencing negative emotions such as jealousy and anger. In other cases, the audience's feelings may not have anything to do with you or your talk. For example, if a colleague is scheduled to present as soon as you finish, he may be so worried about his talk that he can't concentrate on yours. Or perhaps your company is about to announce layoffs; the stress permeating the room will affect your talk.

Assess their level of interest. You will present differently to a highly-engaged group than you will to a bored, clock-watching bunch.

- *High interest level:* When interest is high, you can get right to the point. Include plenty of discussion time because people often want to make comments or ask questions about topics that intrigue them.
- *Mixed interest level:* You might decide to open your talk with a "grabber," a technique that creates interest, as explained on page 61. Also be sure to use a few benefit statements as described on page 19. Or you might try breaking the presentation into two talks; keep the required portion brief with an optional follow-up discussion.
- *Low interest level:* In these cases, your first job is to sell them. Use motivational tools, such as grabbers, benefit statements, and the techniques on pages 17–19. Rather than lecturing, try to involve the audience in some way. Keep your talk brief so they won't feel as if you're wasting their time. And, if you are delivering a sales presentation, act quickly on any attitude changes that occur as a result of your pitch; such changes may not be long-lasting with this type of audience.

2. Determine their probable bias.

You will want to know as soon as possible if the group is likely to be
in favor of your ideas, feel indifferent about them, or be strongly
opposed. Their views may be a result of their values, attitude toward
change, trust in you, or preference for another option. Often, their
bias is also linked to how your request affects them.

Evaluate your request.   Think about what you want the audience to
do as a result of your presentation. Is your request time-consuming,
complicated, or difficult? Or will it be fairly easy to comply with your
request? If you are unclear about what you want, see pages 30–33,
which explain how to set a presentation objective. With this objective
in mind, you will be able to decide whether you are asking for a little
or a lot.

- *Asking for a little:* Even if you are making a simple request that places
  very few demands on your audience, still point out the value of going
  along with your request; explain how attending the talk or accepting your
  recommendation supports their beliefs or benefits them in some way.

- *Asking for a lot:* If you are making a difficult or time-consuming
  request, try one of these techniques: (1) Make the action as easy as
  possible. For example, provide a checklist of new procedures so they
  will be easy to remember. (2) Recognize or reward their effort. For
  instance, if you are asking people to give something up, publicly
  praise their willingness to put the team first.

Analyze their bias.   Using what you know about their emotions
and probable reactions to your request, consider whether your audience's bias will be positive, neutral, or negative. Once you've determined their likely bias, you can plan accordingly.

- *Positive or neutral:* In these cases, state your conclusions or recommendations up front and reinforce their importance. You may also
  want to try briefly presenting and then refuting opposing views to
  "inoculate" the audience against other arguments.

- *Negative:* When their bias is negative, list their possible objections
  and use the techniques on pages 17–19 to influence their views. In par-
  ticular, focus on the ask-for-less appeal and try to build off small agree-
  ments. If their negative feelings are linked to you, see pages 22–23
  for ways to improve your credibility. Also consider meeting with an
  opinion leader before your talk. If you can turn this person into an ally,
  then you will have an easier time getting others to agree with your views.

IV. WHAT WILL PERSUADE THEM?

So far, we've examined who they are, what they know and expect, and what they feel. All this information will be useful as we turn to the last question: What will persuade them? If you are making a recommendation or trying to increase interest, being persuasive is a top priority. Although persuasion is an exceptionally complex topic, we will streamline it for you by providing the ABCs for persuasion: **A**ppeals that address the audience's objections, **B**enefit statements that build support, and **C**redibility tips that focus on you.

1. Appeals that address their objections

Some of the audience's objections may be related to cost, timing, risk, change, effort, practicality, or the desirability of other options. Even an audience with a positive bias will probably have a few concerns. Therefore, no matter what the situation, identify what you think the audience's objections and concerns will be before you put together your presentation. Some particularly effective methods to address these concerns include: bottom-line reasoning, benchmarking efforts, consistency reminders, request adjustments, and limited opportunity appeals.

Bottom-line reasoning: Many decision-makers need to be convinced that costs can be contained, the timing is right, rewards will outweigh risks, change will be profitable, efforts will yield results, and implementation is possible. People who pride themselves on being fact-based and results-oriented will often respond well to such appeals.

   To use bottom-line reasoning, collect reliable data, analyze the numbers, and develop a logical story line. Don't endanger your credibility by taking numbers out of context or by creating misleading charts. To be effective, the data must be credible, the comparisons compelling, and the forecasts realistic. In addition, be prepared to defend your numbers. Check the credibility of your sources, confirm the accuracy of your calculations, and acknowledge the assumptions that guide your arguments.

Benchmarking efforts: Benchmarking involves finding out what others are doing and comparing that data to what your company is doing. If you think the audience will be impressed by the actions or views of others, then benchmarking may prove useful.

Benchmarking is effective only when you use the right comparisons. Compare your organization or project to others that are similar or admirable. For instance, when determining what percentage of the state's budget to allocate for disaster preparedness, a governor may be persuaded by information that shows her state's spending lags far behind that of similarly-sized states.

Communication expert JoAnne Yates concludes "although the fact that 'everyone else is doing it' may not be a very good logical argument, it nevertheless influences some people." For this reason, benchmarking has been labeled "the bandwagon appeal": determine if your comparisons are compelling enough to get your audience to jump on the bandwagon.

Consistency reminders: As persuasion expert Robert Cialdini explains, most people want to be viewed as consistent. As a result, they will continue to back efforts they have publicly and actively supported, especially if they have put those beliefs in writing. For example, if a CEO has put her stamp of approval on the organization's mission statement, she'll feel the pull of consistency if you can show how your recommendation is linked to that mission. Similarly, if you sign a petition that says you support a new recycling program, then you'll have a difficult time saying no to someone who asks you to donate time or money to turn that program into a reality.

Request adjustments: Think about what you are asking of your audience. Sometimes your objective will be so expansive that the audience will object to its scope. Other times, you'll discover that to get their attention, you actually need to increase the size of your request.

- *Ask for less:* Maybe their concern is "it's just too expensive" or "it will drain other resources." In such cases, consider asking for only a small part of what you really want. For example, suggest a pilot program, recommend a trial purchase, or sign up volunteers for a fact-finding committee. Any of these small steps is a way to get your "foot in the door." Once people have given you an initial commitment, you'll have an easier time getting them to agree to future appeals.

• *Ask for more:* Sometimes known as the "door-in-the-face" technique, this tactic is the opposite of the previous one. It has you begin by asking for more than you really want. After the audience objects to your overwhelming request, you find out whether they are willing to accept a small part of it. After all, if you are willing to lessen your demands, it seems fair that they should compromise, too. Fundraisers sometimes use this approach, initially asking for a $5000 donation, but later requesting a more reasonable $500 sum. Clearly, there is a danger in playing the back-and-forth game of reciprocal concessions; if the audience feels no need to work with you, they may simply slam the door.

Limited opportunity appeals: When timing is one of the objections, presenters can point to a "small window of opportunity." Deadlines sometimes persuade people to act without all the information they would normally seek. Similarly, the laws of supply and demand kick in when people learn that something will soon be scarce; the inability to acquire something in the future may make it appear more valuable today. And for many people, there's just a certain caché to that which is uncommon.

2. Benefit statements that build support

One of the standard lessons in sales training involves turning a feature into a benefit. This lesson can be applied to any persuasive presentation. The acronym *WIIFM* stands for "what's in it for me?" Your audience members are eagerly waiting for you to answer this question with a benefit statement.

Creating benefit statements involves three steps. First, identify all the features of a product or an idea. Second, put those features through an "audience filter" to determine which ones actually benefit your audience. Third, generate a benefit statement that clearly and specifically explains what's in it for them.

Step 1: Identify the features.   All products, services, and ideas have many, many features. Features are value-free. They are simply facts about the item or idea you are selling. For example, consider the book you're reading. Here are some of its features: two authors, six chapters, descriptive headings, tips on how to design charts, suggestions for handling speech anxiety, and so on. Some of those features could be turned into a benefit statement for you; others may have little or no value to you.

Identifying the features of an idea tends to be harder than generating features related to a concrete item, such as this book. Nevertheless, try to identify the facts behind your ideas. For example, a real estate professional may discover many facts linked to his idea of relocating corporate headquarters. Those facts may include that his plan: (1) affects the commute of 3500 people, (2) occurs in two phases, (3) can begin next year, (4) involves buying rather than leasing, (5) includes space for an on-site gym, and so on.

Step 2: Apply an "audience filter."   Once you have identified as many features as possible, examine them from the audience's perspective. Think about how people in the audience will respond to each one. You may discover that some of your features will actually lead to objections rather than benefits. For example, while some members of senior management may be thrilled to have an employee gym, others may consider it frivolous. As you apply an audience filter, focus on the features that seem most likely to have a positive effect and those that will be important to the group. Also consider the reaction of people in the secondary audience before you develop specific statements.

Step 3: Create a targeted benefit statement.   Benefit statements clearly explain "what's in it for them." The statements may relate to tangible benefits, such as profits, bonuses, an extra vacation day, or a gift. They may also involve on-the-job benefits, saving people time, simplifying a complex task, reducing errors, or improving morale. In some cases, simply noting how the feature leads to one of these general benefits is enough. At other times, you need to go the next level, creating a detailed statement that makes it exceptionally clear what's in it for them. To make them even more compelling, the WIIFM focus of benefit statements can be combined with other techniques, such as benchmarking or consistency reminders, to form especially powerful, targeted statements.

Returning to the example about moving a company's headquarters, the following table shows how to take a single feature—space for an on-site, employee gym—and turn it into several targeted benefit statements, suitable for different audience members.

TURNING A FEATURE INTO A BENEFIT STATEMENT		
Step 1	**Step 2**	**Step 3**
Identify the feature	**Apply an audience filter**	**Create a targeted benefit statement**
	For an audience member who wants to keep costs under control	For those of you concerned about the bottom line, I want to assure you that the gym's cost can be controlled; we'll actually qualify for lower health-care fees once we provide an on-site fitness facility, which means the gym will pay for itself in three to four years.
The plan includes space for a new gym.	For the decision maker who spoke about the company's concern for employees' health and well-being	As the CEO recently said, "finding time for our health and peace of mind makes us better employees"; this gym is just one more example our CEO can mention at the next employee meeting to show what we're doing to ensure the well-being of our greatest resource—our people.
	For others who want to show their support for the decision maker	
	For an opinion leader who is a yoga enthusiast	The gym offers convenience; even the busiest employees will be able to take stress-reducing yoga classes either over the lunch hour or after work.
	For audience members who are feeling overworked and stressed	

3. Credibility tips that focus on you

Credibility isn't a new concept. Aristotle discussed it more than 2000 years ago, partially defining it as the combination of a speaker's competence and character. As we explained on page 12, your credibility is based on your audience's perception of you, and this perception varies greatly from one situation to the next.

Based on what the audience knows about you and what you've learned about them, figure out which of the following techniques are appropriate for your situation. Be aware that highly-interested and motivated audiences are more likely to be swayed by appeals linked to your content, than by those related to your credibility. However, for less-interested audiences, credibility appeals may be paramount. We've divided these credibility-enhancing tips into two sections: those based on your competence and those linked to your character.

Competence credibility: It's not surprising that if the audience thinks you are competent, they're more likely to accept your opinions. Competence credibility can be associated with everything from the type of information you have on your résumé to the smoothness of your delivery style.

- *Authority:* Sometimes your credibility results from hierarchical power. Having the job of CEO, president, director, or chair may send a signal to some audience members that you deserve their attention because of your role in the organization. Nevertheless, be aware that with some audiences, over-emphasizing your authority can backfire. They may tire of hearing that they should accept ideas just because those ideas have been endorsed by the people in charge.

- *Expertise:* Sometimes your expertise is linked to a title, an accomplishment, or your experience, so be sure they somehow learn that you're a doctor, author, MBA, MPA, or specialist. But expertise is about more than just titles and awards: if you've worked on a project for months, then you may also be viewed as an expert. Likewise, if you've succeeded with other similar projects, then referring to those efforts may bolster your credibility.

- *Associations with experts:* You can also acquire credibility by associating yourself with other people the audience finds competent. Try citing studies done by well-known people at impressive institutions or relating the views of a prominent person. Or, have someone the audience respects introduce you so the audience hears this person's endorsement at the start of your talk.

- *Symbols of competence:* The audience will often link certain symbols to expertise, success, or authority; if you have or wear any of those symbols, then you may acquire some credibility as a result. For instance, gray hair may signal years of experience to some audiences; a uniform with medals may signify authority; or perhaps an expensive watch or designer suit will impress them.

- *Delivery skill:* A polished delivery style can lead the audience to view you as competent—even if your topic has nothing to do with presentation skills. See pages 112–121 for tips on delivery style.

Character credibility: Some credibility appeals concentrate on the audience's perception of your character. Cialdini notes that people prefer to say "yes" to people they know and like. Another element of this type of credibility involves reciprocation and fairness, which has been dubbed "goodwill" by credibility experts French and Raven.

- *Similarity or common ground:* Audiences tend to like speakers they find similar—whether that similarity is reflected in shared values, opinions, needs, experiences, style, or background. Therefore, you can enhance your credibility by referring to a shared experience, mentioning common values or needs, using familiar lingo, or meeting the audience's format and cultural expectations.

- *Good news:* Your audience will be more inclined to like you if you are delivering good news. For example, audiences often respond positively to speakers who compliment them. On the other hand, when speakers are associated with bad news or unpleasant situations, their credibility often suffers.

- *Attractiveness:* Interestingly, many audiences link an attractive image to being both likable and competent. In essence, there is a "halo effect" when a speaker is good looking or well-dressed; it causes people to attribute other positive traits to him or her. Therefore, keeping the audience's expectations in mind, try to dress appropriately and look your best on the day you present.

- *Goodwill:* People often feel a need to reciprocate if you've done them a favor, lent them a hand, or given them a gift. This pattern involves establishing "goodwill." Goodwill credibility also encompasses trustworthiness. For example, if you offer a balanced evaluation of your proposal or acknowledge any potential conflicts of interest, then your audience may see you as fair and trustworthy.

CHAPTER 2 OUTLINE

   I. CONSIDER YOUR GENERAL PURPOSE.
      1. Tell and sell situations
      2. Consult and join situations

  II. WRITE YOUR PRESENTATION OBJECTIVE.
      1. Results-oriented and audience-focused
      2. Specific and measurable
      3. Attainable and worthwhile

 III. USE YOUR OBJECTIVE TO STAY FOCUSED.
      1. When to write your objective
      2. How to use your objective

CHAPTER 2

Identify Your Intent

In addition to thinking about what your audience wants and needs, part of your strategy involves analyzing what you want and need. Therefore, we call a second element of presentation strategy "identifying your intent."

To begin, think about the task you're undertaking and note the general purpose of your talk. Then, narrow your focus until you can create a carefully-crafted statement called a presentation objective. At first glance, constructing these statements won't seem too difficult. But don't be fooled: writing a presentation objective is much tougher than it seems. You'll need to practice to perfect this skill. Once you do, you'll have a talent that makes you far more efficient and focused every time you present.

So, to identify your intent: (1) consider your general purpose, (2) write a presentation objective that specifies what you are trying to accomplish, and (3) use your objective to stay focused as you put together and deliver your talk.

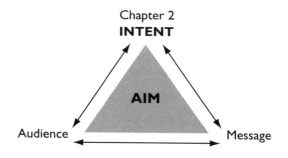

Chapter 2
INTENT

AIM

Audience

Message

I. CONSIDER YOUR GENERAL PURPOSE.

Keeping the audience in mind, think about your task. Perhaps you've been asked to make an announcement or provide an update. In such cases, you already have the information you need and, thus, a high level of control over the content. In other cases, you may need to respond to the audience's concerns or gather information, which means you'll have far less control because these situations require more audience involvement.

As you can see in the diagram below, the information-sharing or "tell" situations at the left are characterized by limited audience participation; you have lots of control in these situations, and you need little, if any, information from the audience. On the other hand, the situations shown at the right are characterized by increased audience interaction and decreased control. Such highly interactive situations focus more on working together or building relationships than on delivering a prepared message.

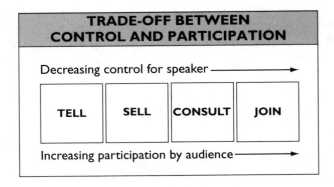

I. Tell and sell situations

Presentations are suited to tell and sell situations—those times when you are an expert or advocate. By their very nature, they give you a fair amount of control over the message and its delivery. Even with lengthy Q&A sessions, they are only moderately interactive.

Tell presentations: If you want to deliver how-to information, welcome new employees, give a progress report, review financial results, or share a memorable moment, you are in a "tell" situation, trying to provide information. Whether your presentation is labeled the weekly update, a financial analysis, a training session, a few opening remarks, or just a story—it is some sort of informative talk.

Most likely, in a tell presentation, you'll determine that your primary task is to explain, inform, review, warn, highlight, update, point out, analyze, compare, or share. If you dig just a bit deeper, you'll uncover your general purpose. For example, perhaps you already know what you want to explain: the rationale for the new dividend policy. Or maybe you've been told what you need to analyze: potential computer security problems. These and other examples of general purposes are listed in the table on the next page.

In reality, most "tell" presentations have a little bit of "sell" in them. For instance, while your general purpose may be to review best practices for campus recruiting, you may also want to encourage the seasoned recruiters to mentor less-experienced personnel. Similarly, if you desire to share your vision for the organization, you may also want to offer several reasons why the audience should embrace your vision.

Sell presentations: When you're pitching a product or trying to change attitudes or behaviors, you're in a "sell" situation. In such cases, you often want your audience to accept your thinking and then do or say something as a result of it. Whether your talk is termed a sales pitch or a motivational message, it's some sort of persuasive presentation.

In such situations, your task may be to influence opinions, initiate change, encourage behavior, recommend a new policy, ensure compliance, thwart the opposition, get their approval, or just persuade them to say "yes." If you add a little more detail, then you will know the general purpose of your presentation. For example, maybe you already know what you want to influence: support for wind power. Or maybe you know what you're trying to thwart: cuts to the research budget. These are just two of the "sell" examples listed in the table below.

When you're selling, it's helpful to have at least some audience involvement. Closing a sale is easier when you can hear the audience's concerns and respond to them, which is why many sales presentations include lots of time for audience members to ask questions. In addition, be aware that in many sales efforts, you'll have to involve your audience emotionally, not just intellectually. To get this involvement, you'll need to give up a little control and use persuasive appeals that go beyond bottom-line reasoning.

EXAMPLES OF GENERAL PURPOSES FOR TELL/SELL SITUATIONS (suited to presentations)	
Types of situations	**Examples of general purposes**
TELL	• Explain rationale for the new dividend policy • Analyze potential computer security problems • Share my vision for the organization • Review "best practices" for campus recruiting • Highlight the elements of my business plan
SELL	• Motivate sales team to build off this year's success • Avoid anticipated cuts to the research budget • Encourage community support for wind power • Pitch our proposal for a new corporate headquarters • Be added to their list of approved suppliers

2. Consult and join situations

Presentations are not suited to those times when you are really a facilitator or moderator. If you are seeking, rather than giving, information, then you are in a consult or join situation.

Consult situations: Preparing a presentation is not the same as planning a meeting because meetings feature audience interaction rather than the delivery of a prepared message. For tips on how to run a meeting, see *Guide to Meetings*, cited on page 137.

When a presentation becomes highly interactive, it's often the result of Q&A. Typically, in Q&A sessions, the speaker has control when explaining the ground rules and while responding to questions. Yet, there are times when Q&A becomes far less controlled. For instance, perhaps the speaker announces: "Since you all want to discuss this topic, let's extend Q&A so you can share your views." In this case, the Q&A is a consult situation.

Join situations: Join situations are even more collaborative. In these cases, other people usually control the message more than you do. For instance, if you were part of a brainstorming session or a team-building retreat, you would be one of several communicators, having little control over many of the messages being sent. These, and the other examples noted below, feature interactive communication.

EXAMPLES OF GENERAL PURPOSES FOR CONSULT/JOIN SITUATIONS (more suited to meetings than presentations)	
Types of situations	**Examples of general purposes**
CONSULT	• Discuss employee turnover • Get reactions to the strategic plan • Share concerns about a new travel policy
JOIN	• Solve technology problem as a group • Negotiate a project schedule and tasks • Brainstorm division goals

II. WRITE YOUR PRESENTATION OBJECTIVE.

In this section we'll explain how to create a presentation objective that is (1) results-oriented and audience-focused, (2) specific and measurable, and (3) attainable and worthwhile.

Writing such an objective benefits you in many ways. For example, it saves you time by preventing you from researching topics you won't end up using or from making dozens of slides no one will ever see. It provides clues about how to open and close your talk. And, if some of your presentation time gets cut, it helps you figure out how to adjust on the spot.

1. Results-oriented and audience-focused

A presentation objective is more than a general statement about your goals or a recap of your presentation's purpose. Instead, it's a statement you create for your own use—one that keeps you on track as you put together and deliver your presentation.

Seek results.   Your presentation objective will only be useful if it actually saves you time and helps you evaluate your efforts. Similarly, a business presentation will only be successful if it accomplishes real results. Therefore, from the very beginning, link your presentation to the results you want to achieve. To do so, start with this phrase: *"As a result of my presentation . . ."*

Focus on the audience.   Although it's easier to think about what you want to say than it is to pinpoint what you are seeking from your audience, the bottom line is that the results you seek are linked to the audience; you want your presentation to affect or influence them in some way. So to maintain an audience focus, continue your objective with the words: *"the audience will . . ."*

Modify the phrase as needed.   You can begin with the exact phrase *"As a result of my presentation, the audience will,"* or you can modify this wording to describe the nature of the talk as shown in the following examples:

"As a result of my sales pitch, the client will . . ."

"As a result of my welcoming remarks, the new employees will . . ."

2. Specific and measurable

You now need to figure out what you want from your audience. To do so, you need to complete the sentence *"As a result of this presentation, the audience will . . ."* with a list of "targets"—which state exactly what you want your audience to think, feel, or do. These targets should be specific and, whenever possible, measurable.

Avoid vague language. For example, if your general purpose is to "highlight the elements of my business plan," then the presentation objective shouldn't be: "As a result of this presentation, the audience will understand the highlights of my business plan." Instead, as a would-be-entrepreneur, you would want to specify which three or four elements you really want to highlight and decide what you mean by "understand." For example, do you want your listeners to be able to describe the talents of the management team to potential investors? Or do you want them to analyze the feasibility of your projections? Or will you be satisfied if they merely recall three important messages about your new venture?

Try to choose measurable targets. Thought- and emotion-based targets are usually hard to measure in a business setting. By comparison, action-based targets are the easiest to evaluate.

- *Understanding is difficult to measure.* Because you can't use final exams or pop quizzes in the workplace, you will have a difficult time measuring what your audience "knows." Unless you have the authority to ask your audience to actually apply or analyze concepts, you may have to settle for identifying the important sound bites and images you want them to hear and see.

- *Emotions are also hard to assess.* In some cases, you can ask people to rate items or share opinions—the way facilitators ask focus group members to record their reactions to speakers, products, or ideas or the way pollsters collect information about preferences and opinions.

- *Actions are the easiest to measure.* Often you will want to specify what you want your audience to "do" or "say." You may decide to have them "complete a sample form" or "authorize a trial purchase." Just make sure the actions you're seeking can be measured as soon as possible after your presentation.

3. Attainable and worthwhile

Your presentation objective should include several targets. Rank their importance and assess their difficulty. Knowing which ones are the most important will help you decide which ones to keep.

Make sure your objective is attainable.   Typically, people think they can cover many more topics or achieve many more results than possible with a single presentation. To avoid this trap, critique your objective by considering how much time you'll really have, factoring in the receptivity of the audience and acknowledging the limitations associated with giving a presentation.

- *Be realistic about timing.* Consider the time you'll need for introductions, the time you'll spend handling questions, and so on. Estimate the actual time you'll have to accomplish your presentation objective.
- *Use audience analysis insight.* If, for example, you need to build interest or overcome a negative bias, then you will have less time to accomplish your objective.
- *Know what's possible.* Many things you say will not, in fact, be heard and remembered, which is why you can't highlight 10 major points in a presentation.

Make sure your objective is worthwhile.   Once you become skilled at creating presentation objectives, another issue may surface: they can become too straightforward.

Consider this easy-to-measure objective: "As a result of my presentation, the audience will agree to include us on their approved supplier list." Although it meets the criteria reviewed so far, this objective wouldn't help you decide what to include in your pitch. To make it more useful: (1) Identify key messages (by inserting benefit statements or specifying take-away points) or (2) Include "supplemental targets" (which might refer to attitudes or emotions.) Although tough to evaluate, emotion-based targets don't have to be excluded. If they help you focus, add them as supplemental targets.

The table on the facing page lists objectives that are both attainable and worthwhile.

FROM GENERAL PURPOSES TO PRESENTATION OBJECTIVES	
General purpose	**Presentation objective**
Explain the rationale for the new dividend policy (TELL)	As a result of my presentation, the analysts will hear that we've changed our dividend policy for three reasons: (1) investor attitude has moved toward a yield preference; (2) our continued level of surplus capital made it impractical to continue the current payout ratio; (3) two recent changes to Australian tax law make our new policy more desirable.
Share my vision for the organization (TELL)	*Presentation objective:* As a result of my presentation, the VPs will . . . 1. Explain to their direct reports that: (a) innovation involves embracing risk and accepting false starts and (b) managing people effectively is both cost-effective and culture-effective. 2. See what I hope our company will look like 10 years from today: an image that features more than two dozen new products on display in our conference rooms and familiar faces throughout the ranks of senior management. *Supplemental target:* The audience will feel proud of our past innovations and be inspired by anecdotes about the contributions of great managers.
Motivate the sales team to build off this year's success (SELL)	*Presentation objective:* As a result of my presentation at the regional sales meeting, the employees will: 1. Give their applause to our six associates who received awards and turned in top performances. 2. Find out that we met our goal and expanded market share by .24%. 3. Hear the three new positioning messages we'll roll out next quarter. 4. Review a list of promotional tools and compare the number available to the number they currently use. *Supplemental target:* They will feel proud to be part of a successful team and use some new tools to achieve even better results next year.
Be added to their list of approved suppliers (SELL)	As a result of this sales pitch, their purchasing department will: 1. Hear that Lite Gauge Metals has (a) a reputation for on-time delivery, which means they won't need to hold excess inventory and (b) the ability to slit wide-width coils, which means they can reduce lead times for their 55" material. 2. See product samples that verify the precision of our machinery and review packaging protocols that explain why our material arrives without dings or scratches. 3. Agree to add us to their approved supplier list and ask us to provide quotes for at least two different specs this quarter.

III. USE YOUR OBJECTIVE TO STAY FOCUSED.

Your presentation objective will help you throughout the presentation process—from the early stages when you are thinking about the audience and researching your topic to the final moments when you are closing your talk.

I. When to write your objective

You will be more efficient if you draft your presentation objective before you do substantial research. Although audience and intent both need to be considered early in the presentation process, different people like to proceed in different ways. In most cases, you will need to be flexible as you approach strategy; you may discover that you'll need to modify your presentation objective before you determine what you'll say.

Draft your objective early in the process.   Some people draft a presentation objective before they do anything else. Others begin with audience analysis and then move to intent, using a system that mirrors the sequence of this book. And still others use their general purpose as a springboard to collect information and then write their presentation objective. If you are having trouble drafting your presentation objective, use a mind map or the nutshell technique to help you get started.

- *Using a mind map:* This tool is popular with random thinkers. It can help them focus, generate, and synthesize information. You will find information about mind maps on pages 54 and 59.
- *Trying the nutshell technique:* Another tool to help you focus, the nutshell technique, is described on page 56.

Make modifications as needed.   Situations change, and your presentation objective may need to change, too. For example, you may discover a new computer virus is crippling computers in other parts of the world, so your warning about computer security now needs to focus on how to prevent this specific hazard. Or you may learn that people outside the company plan to attend your presentation so you can no longer include and highlight confidential information. Although the presentation objective is supposed to keep you on track as you determine what you'll say, it's fine to make adjustments as you discover new information.

2. How to use your objective

Your presentation objective keeps you focused as you prepare and present. It also enables you to determine your success.

As you prepare: Keep your objective in mind as you put together your talk. Consider it when you . . .

- *Prepare your opening and closing:* As explained on pages 38–40, the first and last parts of your presentation are most likely to be remembered; therefore, make sure your opening and closing are linked to your presentation objective in some way.

- *Decide what to highlight:* If your presentation objective identifies a sound bite that you want the audience to hear, use one or more of the highlighting techniques described on pages 41–43 to ensure this message gets emphasized.

- *Design your visual aids:* Not all your information can or should be included on your visual aids. As explained on pages 82–83, your slides, deck pages, or handouts should emphasize what's important, and much of what's important is the information that helps you accomplish your objective.

As you rehearse and present: Your presentation objective helps you determine what to cut and what to emphasize. After a timed rehearsal, you may discover you have too much information; if so, a clearly defined presentation objective shows you what to eliminate. Your objective also helps you stay on track when you are answering questions or running overtime. For example, if a question is related to your presentation objective, then you'll want to comment on it thoroughly, making your response of interest to the whole group. On the other hand, if a question is not linked to your objective, then you'll want to address it quickly, but not allow it to sidetrack you from what you are trying to accomplish.

To evaluate your success: You made sure your objective was measurable for a reason: so you can evaluate your efforts. Just because your boss said "Hey, you looked good up there!" doesn't mean your presentation was a success. Similarly, a momentary stammer or audiovisual glitch doesn't doom you to presentation failure. Remember, the way you succeed is by setting a good presentation objective and then meeting it.

CHAPTER 3 OUTLINE

I. MAKE YOUR MESSAGE MEMORABLE.
1. Harness the power of beginnings and endings.
2. Chunk your content.
3. Use highlighting techniques.

II. CONSIDER THE MEDIUM.
1. Compare presentations to other options.
2. Supplement your presentation with another medium.

CHAPTER 3

Make the Most of the Message

Now that we've addressed audience and intent, we'll focus on the third part of AIM: message strategy. Although the term "message" has many meanings, as part of the AIM model, it refers to the content of your presentation: what you include in your talk, how you structure this content, and how you emphasize the points you want to make. It also refers to the "medium" you are using to deliver your content—in this case, a presentation.

The medium influences how information is received by your audience, which is one reason that "message strategy" is connected to "audience strategy." In addition, "message" is very closely linked to "intent"—your objective should be suited to the medium you are using, and it should clearly identify the content you wish to emphasize.

This chapter explains how to make the most of the message. To do so: (1) use techniques to make your content memorable and (2) make sure that a presentation is, in fact, the right medium to use.

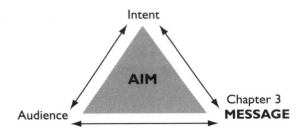

I. MAKE THE MESSAGE MEMORABLE.

Although your audience may try to listen to all your data, examples, facts, and opinions, in reality, they can only take in and recall a small portion of what you say. As the speaker, it's your job to help them hear, see, and remember your important points. To make your message memorable, (1) harness the power of the beginnings and endings, (2) "chunk" your content, and (3) use highlighting techniques.

1. Harness the power of beginnings and endings.

Audience attention tends to be high when you begin your presentation, but, as you continue, attention may wander. Some people tune in and out, others fall prey to long bouts of daydreaming, and still others get more involved with text messaging than they do with your talk. Nevertheless, when you say something such as "to wrap up . . ." or "so, in conclusion . . ." most audience members perk up. They listen intently, hoping to find out what they missed along the way.

Not surprisingly, how your audience listens also affects what they remember. The Audience Memory Curve, shown below, is a graphic representation of a well-known principle (sometimes known as the "primacy/recency effect"): people tend to recall what's first and last, not what's in the middle. This principle means the audience is likely to (1) remember what you say during the opening and closing parts of your presentation and (2) recall the first and last items in each bullet list more than those in the middle.

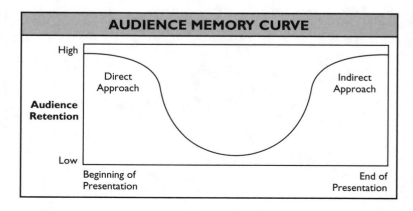

AUDIENCE MEMORY CURVE

High

Direct Approach

Indirect Approach

Audience Retention

Low

Beginning of Presentation

End of Presentation

To harness the power of the beginning, emphasize your conclusions by using what's known as a "direct approach" whenever possible. If the audience or message makes this option problematic, then use an indirect approach instead.

Emphasize conclusions.   Your conclusions should be in the opening or closing of your talk. If you share them fully in the opening, you will be using a "direct approach."

- *Direct approach:* The direct approach states your conclusions clearly from the onset, so the audience knows your bottom line before they listen to your explanations, details, or arguments. When the audience hears your conclusion first, they have a much easier time following your supporting ideas.

- *Indirect approach:* By contrast, the indirect approach saves the most important conclusions for the end. This approach is like a mystery story: it takes a long time for the audience to determine where all the evidence is leading.

Use the direct approach whenever possible.   Although it may seem counter-intuitive to share your conclusions first, most business audiences prefer this approach because it . . .

- *Improves comprehension and saves time:* People assimilate content more readily when they know the conclusions first. Surprise endings are fine for mystery readers, but not for busy executives who may resent every minute they spend trying to figure out what you're trying to say. The direct approach communicates your position more quickly and effectively than an indirect one.

- *Focuses on the audience's interests more than your discovery process:* The direct approach emphasizes the results of your analysis. By contrast, an indirect one reviews the steps of your analysis. Although many audience members may want to hear about the scope of your project or the ideas that guided your efforts, most will care far more about your final results than about how you discovered them. With a direct approach, you focus on their interests rather than your methodology.

The direct approach is appropriate for all non-sensitive messages. In addition, it's a good choice for sensitive messages if (1) the audience has a positive or neutral bias, (2) they are results-oriented, or (3) your credibility is high. In the United States, chances are you should be using the direct approach more than 90 percent of the time.

Use an indirect approach with caution. Since the indirect approach is harder to follow and takes longer to understand, use it with care. In some situations, it may prevent the audience from disagreeing with you right away, soften their resistance to an unpopular idea, or increase their tendency to view you as fair-minded. Nevertheless, use this approach only when certain constraints require you to do so . . .

- *Audience and message constraints:* when you have (1) a highly sensitive message, low credibility, and a negatively-biased or a hostile audience, or (2) an analysis-oriented decision maker who insists upon it.
- *Cultural constraints:* when you are presenting in another culture in which the direct approach would be viewed as inappropriate or pushy.

2. "Chunk" your content.

Another way to help people grasp important ideas is to limit how many you include. Psychology experiments have shown that people can't easily remember more than five to seven items. This finding does not mean that you should stand up, make five points, and then sit down. Rather, it explains why you need to learn how to organize information so that it's easier to recall.

Chunking improves recall. Packaging information into sections, or chunking it, dramatically improves attention and retention. Therefore, you may be able to cover dozens of topics in your presentation if you can find ways to categorize them. Identify your major concepts. Figure out how they are related. Then chunk them into the main sections of your presentation.

Although many people can remember seven items on a list, don't make your listeners work so hard: use anywhere from two to five main sections in your presentation, then divide those sections into a limited number of subsections.

Chunking creates mini-memory curves. A major benefit of packaging information in sections is that by doing so, you can add emphatic locations to the Audience Memory Curve. Instead of having one long curve with a big dip, you create several mini-memory curves, each with its own dip and peaks. In essence, chunking elevates overall attention and gives you more opportunities to emphasize important points.

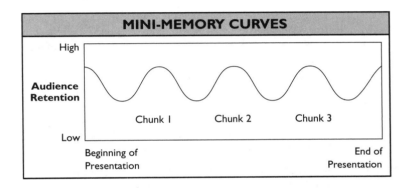

Chunking enables you to create a "preview." A preview (or "agenda") explains the structure of your talk. These statements are extremely important for your audience, because listeners, unlike readers, can't flip back and see what they missed. Instead, they rely on what you tell them about the sections, or chunks, that make up your presentation's structure.

All presentations need a preview, but before you can create one, you'll need to identify and label the sections of your talk. See pages 61 and 63 for more details and examples of previews.

3. Use highlighting techniques.

In addition to relying on the power of beginnings and endings and chunking the content, you can also use other techniques to emphasize information. This section identifies seven highlighting tools that can capture the audience's attention and make your message memorable.

Repetition gets noticed.   People remember what they hear or see several times, so one way to highlight a point is to repeat it.

- *Say your sound bite more than once:* If you have a catchy statement you want the audience to recall, say it more than once. Or repeat that idea in another way, perhaps adding an example or showing an image that makes the same point.

- *Always repeat to reinforce structure:* You can also use repetition to reinforce your presentation's structure. The preview you include in your opening uses this technique: the audience hears the sections you'll be covering during your opening and then once again when you begin each section. Transitional statements, as explained on page 64, also use repetition to reinforce structure.

Flagging signals importance.   The technique of "flagging" is easy to use. You simply draw attention to important points by using a verbal flag, such as "If you remember only one thing, remember . . ." or "Here's the critical point." No matter which words or phrases you use as a flag, they should signal that an important idea is coming up next.

The unexpected grabs attention.   People tend to remember something that is unusual or unexpected—called "the Von Restorff effect," after the psychologist who researched this phenomenon. By using a surprise or attention-getting change in your presentation, you can focus the audience's attention on a point that would otherwise be lost. For example, try telling a startling story, dramatically changing your delivery style, showing a powerful video clip, or altering the pace of your presentation in a humorous or unexpected way.

Yet, here's the caveat: with both flagging and the Von Restorff effect, the more you use these techniques, the less emphasis each use will have. Even more problematic, a surprise or change that is seen as too gimmicky may damage your credibility and, at the same time, make this damaging moment very memorable.

Visuals provide reinforcement. During a presentation, the presenter is the most important visual; nevertheless, well-designed visuals can also make a presentation more memorable. If people see a message as they listen to it, they are more likely to retain it. To apply the Von Restorff effect further, if one visual is different than all the rest (for instance, a photograph rather than ubiquitous bullet lists), then the unusual visual will be the one that's remembered.

Involvement adds interest. Because people tend to drift off as they listen, you may want to involve the audience so they're doing more than just listening: ask them to think about a single question or discuss a relevant point; have them participate in an exercise or demonstration; give them a chance to talk to each other by forming "buzz groups"; or set up some other type of group activity. Although such activities take time away from your prepared content, they can help you achieve your objective. Typically, audiences recall what they heard, saw, and experienced when they were highly engaged.

Breaks help people focus. If you're planning a long presentation, understand the value of scheduling a break. Most people can't sit and listen for two hours; in fact, research shows that people tend to lose concentration after 50 minutes without a break. So, you will get more accomplished if you devote at least 15 minutes of your two-hour talk to a break. If used properly, a break turns a long talk into two manageable presentations, giving you more opportunities to position important messages at the beginning and the ending. Schedule breaks so they come between (not in the middle of) main points.

Mnemonics assist memory. These devices have long been used to help people retain information. Some are rhymes, while others use visual and auditory links to improve memory. One common type, an acronym, makes a word out of the first letters of items in a list. For example, we use the acronym AIM to stress that strategy involves **A** (Audience), **I** (Intent), and **M** (Message). Since AIM summarizes our entire approach to presentation strategy, we hope this mnemonic device makes the concept more memorable.

II. CONSIDER THE MEDIUM.

Always be sure that a presentation is the best medium (or "channel") to use.

I. Compare presentations to other options.

You have many channel choices. You can write a letter, pick up the phone, set up a conference call, deliver a presentation, and so on. In this section, we'll offer some tips about choosing the most effective channel.

Variations among the options: Some of the choices are written and others are spoken. Some reach groups, while others target individuals. In addition, some are no tech or low tech, while others rely on new technology and remind us that even more sophisticated options are likely on the way.

- *Written versus spoken:* Written options include emails, memos, reports, and text messages, while spoken ones include phone calls, meetings, panel discussions, and presentations, just to name a few. Unlike most spoken options, written media create a permanent record, and many are capable of delivering detailed messages that can be easily edited. But writing doesn't include nonverbal elements, such as vocal traits or body language.

- *Group versus individual:* In addition to presentations, group media include conference calls, meetings, websites, and blogs. These are less private than meeting with an individual, phoning someone, or sending a personal letter.

- *High tech versus low tech:* High-tech alternatives include video-conferences, electronic meeting systems (EMS), web pages, and web-casts, while low-tech options include face-to-face conversations and traditional written correspondence. Using technology can add "noise" or elements that distort both verbal and nonverbal messages. For example, videoconferences can include static that interferes with vocal cues and camera shots that make facial expression hard to see. Nevertheless, high-tech options enable people in different locations to communicate more rapidly than they could with low-tech ones.

A presentation, then, is a spoken, group medium that is traditionally low tech, but one that can be supplemented with high-tech visual aids or written materials.

Channel-choice checklist: What you know about your audience and intent should influence whether you give a presentation. Other factors—such as privacy, logistical considerations, cost, and your content—may also play a role. Use these questions to assess your options:

1. *Does your audience have a preference?* If your boss or client tells you that you are giving a presentation, then chances are, you're giving a presentation. In other situations, the decision may be up to you. If so, assess the audience's preference and consider the advantages and disadvantages of using that medium.

2. *How much audience participation do you want?* Presentations are suited to tell and sell situations, which offer lots of control, but limited audience interaction. If you want higher levels of participation, include a Q&A session in your talk. If you need even more participation, arrange a meeting instead.

3. *Do you want nonverbal, as well as verbal, communication?* (1) If nonverbal messages and interaction aren't important, then you may be able to communicate in writing, which is less expensive in terms of audience time. (2) If vocal cues would be helpful, but body language isn't important, then present using a teleconference. (3) If rich nonverbal cues are important, then choose a face-to-face medium, such as a presentation, which offers these elements. Nonverbal elements like prolonged eye contact, a clear vocal tone, and a firm handshake can help establish credibility, build relationships, and correct miscommunication.

4. *Do you want to control the timing of the message and response?* Consider whether you need to know exactly when your message will be received or to control when, or even if, you will get a response. Face-to-face options offer the most control over these factors.

5. *Do you want a permanent record?* Written and recorded efforts leave documentation. If you need to retransmit your message, then an electronic record will be helpful. If you don't want a record, avoid written channels and opt for unrecorded telephone or face-to-face interactions.

6. *How much detail do you want to communicate?* Writing can include charts, tables, diagrams, and photographs as well as words. You can include a great deal of detail in a written report or on a website; if you tried to include the same level in a presentation or meeting, much of it would be lost since people can process more information through their eyes (reading) than through their ears (listening).

7. *Do you need to control costs?* Meetings and presentations frequently cost more than people realize, especially if the event is held at an off-site facility. To reduce the expense, some people opt to write, while others choose to meet or present using video or teleconferences.

Presentation advantages and disadvantages: Each medium involves trade-offs, whether you're giving up some control to get more participation or whether you're sacrificing privacy so that many people can hear the same information at the same time. The following table identifies several features of a presentation and explains the benefits and drawbacks of each feature.

PRESENTATIONS: ADVANTAGES AND DISADVANTAGES		
Presentation feature	**Advantages**	**Disadvantages**
High control of content/ low audience involvement	• Meets your needs when you're an expert or advocate wanting to inform or persuade • Provides control over what content is addressed and how and when it is delivered	• Fails to meet your needs when you want to gather information, work as a team, and so on • Limits audience participation, which can lower interest level and attention
No record (unless recorded or supplemented with handouts or copies of slides)	• Limits information leaks • Can be supplemented with slides or handouts to provide a record	• Makes it hard for people who didn't attend to find out what they missed • Allows information leaks (if the supplemental materials include confidential information)
Face-to-face and group medium (speaker and audience are in the same place at the same time; includes nonverbal messages)	• Enhances verbal messages with rich nonverbal cues • Enables speaker to make clarifications right away • Allows the speaker to seek an immediate response and to determine success based on the presentation objective • Saves time compared to a series of one-to-one meetings • Gets people out of their offices and focused on your talk	• Limits detail because listeners can't process or review material like readers • Prevents speaker from avoiding angry audience members • Allows decision makers to say "no" in a public forum, which makes it harder to influence their views later • May involve scheduling problems or high costs • Lacks privacy, making it difficult to deliver sensitive or hard-to-hear messages to specific audience members

2. Supplement your presentation with another medium.

If a presentation alone won't accomplish everything you want, then consider supplementing it with another medium. For example, if you add written materials, you will be able to include detailed information or document your talk. Likewise, if you need more interaction, then maybe you will choose to include a Q&A session. Or maybe you will want to think of your presentation as part of a larger effort, using other types of communication before and after your talk. All these possibilities enable you to capitalize on some of the advantages of giving a presentation and overcome a few of the drawbacks.

Adding written materials: Writing has several advantages over speaking. (1) It's suited to complex information because it can be viewed and reviewed at the recipient's own pace. (2) It leaves a record that can be saved in a computer or filing cabinet. (3) If electronic, it can be easily and inexpensively distributed to a large audience.

If you choose to supplement your presentation with written documents, you can use them as background material sent before your talk, pass them out during your talk, or distribute them after the presentation, either to provide additional information to interested audience members or to serve as a permanent record. Two common types of presentation materials are handouts and decks.

- *Handouts:* If you need to discuss complex financial information, you might distribute a spreadsheet at the point in your presentation when you are discussing those numbers—instead of projecting a table of microscopic type on your slide. You might also use handouts as background material—distributing reports, articles, or websites before your talk. Or you might want to prepare take-away handouts, such as lists of resources, articles you referenced, or brochures about your organization, service, or product.

- *Decks:* See page 81 for more information about this common visual aid, which can be used in different ways: (1) Decks may be the primary visual, in which case, the speaker and audience move though the printed material together. (2) At other times, they are used along with projected slides. In these instances, the presentation deck may simply be printed copies of all the slides, with or without additional material. Such decks may be distributed before the talk (enabling the audience to use them for taking notes), or after the talk to provide a record of the presentation.

Including some interaction: Q&A sessions make your presentation more interactive. Sometimes audience members ask questions throughout your talk, and sometimes Q&A takes place after your prepared remarks. These sessions can be low-key exchanges or very spirited debates. So when you are thinking about what you want to say to your audience, also consider whether you want to include Q&A, and if so, how you want to handle it; see pages 67–75 for more information on how to do so.

Layering your communication efforts: You may not want to think of a presentation as an isolated event; many times it will be one link in a larger chain of communication. For all sorts of reasons, you might choose to combine several efforts, using one after the other. For example, you might decide that your objective is too complex to be accomplished with a single presentation or you might fear that you're going to face a hostile audience. Just analyzing an unknown audience will probably require you to use another medium to collect the strategic information needed to prepare your talk.

- *When the presentation should be the last step:* If you want to make a big change, like restructuring your organization, then schedule a series of information-gathering meetings before your presentation; you will want to learn what others think and discuss their concerns before you prepare your presentation.

- *When a presentation is just the first step:* Sometimes, you won't have enough time to accomplish your presentation objective in one presentation. In such cases, consider piggybacking several efforts to achieve the results you're seeking. Consider using follow-up presentations, meetings, or written reports.

- *When the audience has a negative bias:* If you fear you'll be confronted by a hostile audience, then try arranging private meetings with influential audience members before your talk. Listen carefully to their objections and views. Try to uncover areas of mutual agreement and get a modicum of support before you present to the group; once the group hears that people they respect share some of your views, you'll have an easier time with those who oppose your efforts.

- *When you need to do extensive audience analysis:* If you're analyzing an unknown audience, you will probably need to layer channels as part of your AIM strategy. For example, to learn about a large, unknown group, you might need to send emails, pick up the phone, and then meet with someone who's familiar with the group.

Once you've confirmed that a presentation is, in fact, the right communication medium for your situation, you can move from strategy to the implementation phase, as discussed in the second half of the book. But never forget to base that implementation on your AIM strategy: audience, intent, and message.

PART II

Implementation Framework

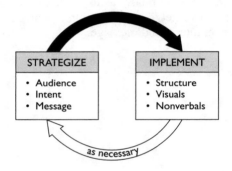

PART II

Presentation Implementation

When most people think about giving a presentation, they tend to focus on the implementation skills we will cover in Part II: What will I say? What slides should I use? How will I look and sound? We hope we have persuaded you by now that you should AIM before you start preparing your presentation. Strategy should always drive implementation. For example, your audience should influence your nonverbal delivery; your credibility should affect what you decide to say; your intent should determine what appears on your visual aids.

The diagram for Part II, shown on the facing page, illustrates this concept: the black arrow represents your strategy driving your implementation. However, because we don't want to imply that this is a lockstep process—first you set your strategy, then you implement it—we use the white arrow pointing left to remind you to refer back to your strategy, as necessary, while you . . .

- Structure the Content (Chapter 4)
- Design the Visuals (Chapter 5)
- Refine Your Nonverbal Delivery (Chapter 6)

CHAPTER 4 OUTLINE

   I. COLLECT, FOCUS, AND ORDER INFORMATION.
      1. Collect strategic and topical information.
      2. Focus what you've collected.
      3. Order the content.

   II. DECIDE WHAT TO SAY.
      1. Decide how you'll open.
      2. Prepare a well-organized body.
      3. Determine how you'll close.

   III. PREPARE FOR Q&A.
      1. Get ready for their questions.
      2. Refine your listening skills.
      3. Respond effectively.
      4. Listen for challenging questions.
      5. Control difficult or hostile audience members.

CHAPTER 4

Structure the Content

Your presentation strategy (AIM) should influence what you say during your presentation. To structure your content: (1) collect, focus, and order information; (2) decide what to say during the opening, body, and closing of your talk; and (3) think about how you will answer any questions your audience might ask.

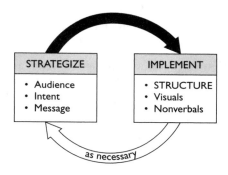

I. COLLECT, FOCUS, AND ORDER INFORMATION.

An effective presentation is based on accurate and appropriate information; therefore, follow these steps as you consider the content of your talk.

1. Collect strategic and topical information.

To collect information about your strategy and your topic: (1) determine what you know and (2) research to learn more.

Determine what you already know.   Often you will know a lot about both the topic and your audience; even when the subject matter is new and the audience is unfamiliar, chances are you'll have at least some awareness of the subject and the situation.

- *Review your strategy.* List what you already know about the four audience analysis questions outlined in Chapter 1. Identify your general purpose and write your presentation objective as described in Chapter 2. In addition, think about the benefits and drawbacks of giving a presentation to make sure you're using the right medium for your message, as discussed in Chapter 3.

- *Do a topical data dump.* List relevant facts about your topic and identify some of the resources you want to consult. Round up the data, images, and files you want to reexamine. Make notations about your ideas and the ideas of others that will guide your approach.

- *Try a mind map.* A mind map is a way to collect and focus topical information all at once. This technique has you (1) write your purpose in the middle of a large sheet of paper and circle it; (2) jot down ideas that are related to what you've put in the circle, using words, phrases, or even simple drawings to quickly capture what you know; and (3) draw lines to connect ideas that are linked. Mind mapping appeals the most to people who are random thinkers. It's a fast, messy way to generate ideas so you can see some possible order in all your free-flowing thoughts, as illustrated on page 59. You can learn more about mind mapping by reading Tony Buzan's book, listed in the bibliography on page 136.

Research to learn more. You will probably be researching both strategic and topical information. In your audience analysis efforts, you may be calling people familiar with the group, emailing several audience members for their opinions, or learning more about where people work by checking out a website or company brochure.

You can also research topical information in various ways. Some people like to work with colleagues who can help them collect and interpret data. Others prefer solitary research—reading articles, studying spreadsheets, surfing the web, or looking through files. Some of the following tips may make your research time more productive:

- *Telephone tips:* If you're calling someone for information, clarify your questions before you phone. Ask clear questions and take notes as you listen so you won't need to repeat the call. If you're leaving a message, be brief, but provide a general idea of what information you're seeking. Although this last tip may also seem very obvious, consider how many times you've had to replay someone's voice mail message: remember to speak slowly when saying your name and phone number and repeat the number so the listener won't need to replay your message.

- *Email tips:* Since most people are inundated with email messages, make your message polite and easy to read. Compose a clear, brief message for the subject line that will appear in the reader's inbox. Make it clear, both from the subject line and the opening of your email message, that you are requesting information. Introduce yourself, if necessary. Let the recipient know when you need the information and keep your message short so that the reader won't have to scroll down to read your request.

- *Internet tips:* General Internet searches often turn up thousands of hits unless you know how to narrow your request. All search engines and subject directories have their own idiosyncrasies about how to focus a search. For good tips on how to navigate the web, check out the Internet tutorial created at UC Berkeley: http.lib.berkeley.edu/TeachingLib/Guides/Internet/FindInfo.html. This site even explains how to find "the invisible web." If you don't have time to become an Internet maven, at least spend some time learning more about how to use various search engines. For example, if you're using Google, check out their tip sheet at www.google.com/help/cheatsheet.html.

2. Focus what you've collected.

You now need to filter the information you've gathered so you can make necessary adjustments and synthesize what you've collected.

Filter the information.   Using your AIM strategy to guide you, apply both an audience and an intent filter to clarify your focus.

- *The audience filter:* Review what you know about the audience's knowledge, their expectations, and their feelings as discussed in Chapter 1. Also think about what information might influence their views and which ideas may help you create statements that explain "what's in it for them."

- *The intent filter:* Use your objective to separate what is on target from what's not necessary. Some presenters like to post their objective near their computer or on the wall above their desk so they can keep their eye on it while collecting and focusing information.

Adjust as necessary.   Perhaps some of the information seems inappropriate for your audience or unrelated to your presentation objective. If so, you'll either need to collect more information or make adjustments. If you have the authority, you might want to add or subtract people from your audience. For example, if you have one expert and many novices in your audience, you might warn the expert that she'll find the presentation too basic for her needs or you might want to ask her if she would like to assist you in presenting some of the material. In other cases, you may decide that you need to redo your presentation objective. If you haven't been able to craft a satisfactory presentation objective, as described in Chapter 2, then try to focus your ideas in another fashion, perhaps trying the nutshell technique that follows.

"Nutshell" the information.   Stand back from the information you've collected and try to summarize it. Imagine you are trying to communicate the essence of your presentation in a very short time.

- *The elevator technique:* Pretend you have the decision maker's attention for 90 seconds, perhaps sharing an elevator ride down to the lobby: What messages would you most want to share with this person? What would you ask for at the end of your comments?

- *The email technique:* Assume you have to explain the gist of your presentation in a short email. How would you briefly describe your point of view? What key take-away messages would you include?

3. Order the content.

To organize the pertinent information you've collected, find a method for grouping similar ideas so you can discover the "chunks" of information that you will include in your presentation.

Using an outline: If you think in a very linear, fashion and you can easily distinguish major themes from secondary points, then you will probably prefer to organize your ideas with an outline: either a traditional one (using Roman numerals and capital letters) or an informal one (using bullet points and dashes). As we discussed in Chapter 3, limit the number of major sections in your outline and order your points in a way that will seem logical to the audience and help you accomplish your presentation objective.

Making an idea chart: Frequently used by consultants, idea charts are more visual than outlines. To create an idea chart: (1) list your important ideas, (2) find ways to group them into a limited number of categories, and (3) label each group. If constructed like a pyramid, your main idea will be in a box at the top of the pyramid, with your main sections placed below it, as illustrated on the following page. For more information about how to construct idea charts, refer to Barbara Minto's book in the bibliography on page 137.

Starting with a storyboard: This ordering method may prove useful for visual thinkers. To create a storyboard: (1) start with a series of blank boxes that represent possible slides; (2) create a preview slide that identifies the sections of your talk or save this step for later if necessary; (3) sketch the images you want to highlight in each box; (4) write important messages as titles; and (5) number the boxes to show the sequence. Create your storyboard with pencil and paper, not in PowerPoint, where you may waste time perfecting slides that you later decide to delete.

Using your own method: If the above suggestions don't seem helpful, then find a method that works for you. For example, you might try using a combination of mind mapping, as described on page 54, and sticky notes. Aided by these tools, you could use the mind map to identify your most important ideas and then transfer those ideas to sticky notes. The notes could then be moved around until they form an idea chart that shows how to order your talk.

IDEA CHART EXAMPLES

"Data dump" of all gathered information
Eliminate product X.
Provide *pro formo* statements.
Redefine departmental responsibilities.
Decrease capital expenditures.
Expand marketing division.
Concentrate on product Y.
Renegotiate short-term liability.

Idea chart organizing the information shown above

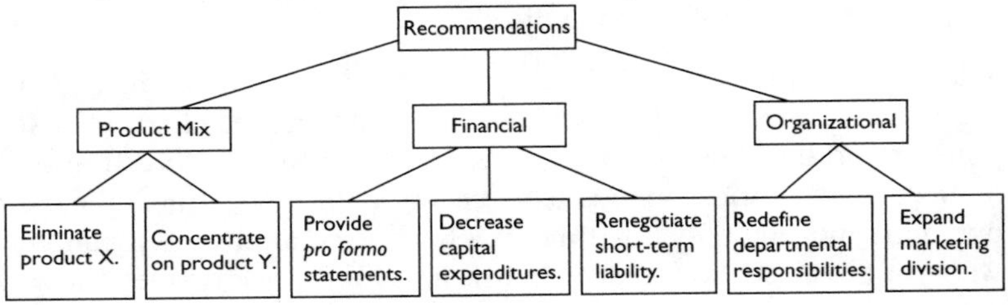

Recommendations

Product Mix — Financial — Organizational

Eliminate product X. | Concentrate on product Y. | Provide *pro formo* statements. | Decrease capital expenditures. | Renegotiate short-term liability. | Redefine departmental responsibilities. | Expand marketing division.

Other typical idea charts

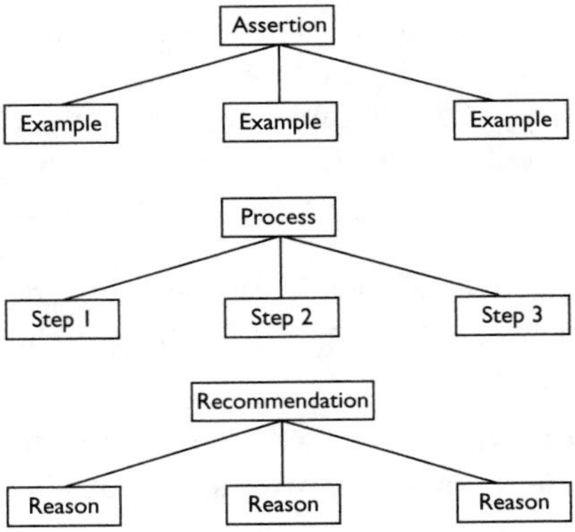

Assertion

Example | Example | Example

Process

Step 1 | Step 2 | Step 3

Recommendation

Reason | Reason | Reason

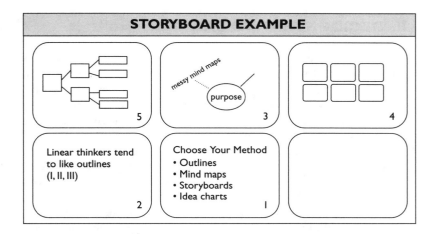

STORYBOARD EXAMPLE

messy mind maps .... purpose   5   3   4

Linear thinkers tend to like outlines (I, II, III)   2

Choose Your Method
• Outlines
• Mind maps
• Storyboards
• Idea charts   I

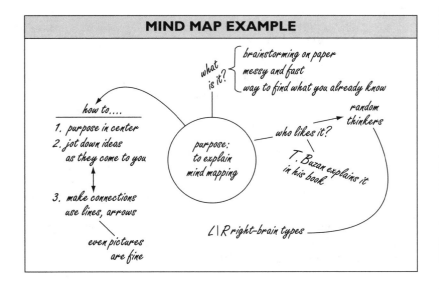

MIND MAP EXAMPLE

what is it?
{ *brainstorming on paper*
messy and fast
way to find what you already know }

how to....
1. *purpose in center*
2. *jot down ideas as they come to you*
3. *make connections use lines, arrows*
even pictures are fine

purpose: to explain mind mapping

random thinkers
who likes it?
T. Buzan explains it in his book

L \ R right-brain types

II. DECIDE WHAT TO SAY.

Once you've researched, focused, and ordered the information, it's time to turn that material into a presentation. In this section, we'll explain how to decide what you'll actually say in each part of your talk.

Like a written document, a presentation has three parts: the opening, the body, and the closing. But, unlike a written document, a presentation needs a structure that is repetitive and exceptionally clear. Listeners aren't like readers: they can't glance back to refresh their memories or skip ahead to check out the end. So when you are giving a presentation, always include a preview that outlines the sections you plan to cover, and use explicit transitions that remind your listeners about what you just covered and what you plan to talk about next.

Prepare the opening, body, and closing in any sequence that works for you. Some people like to start with the body and their preview to ensure a clear structure. Others prefer to use a chronological approach, first deciding how to open, then preparing the body, and finally determining how to close.

1. Decide how you'll open.

Your opening is crucial. It sets the stage, builds interest in your topic, and explains the structure of your talk. Although there are several tasks to accomplish with the opening, don't make this section too long or complex; be sure you get to your preview well before the audience wonders where you are headed with your talk.

Set the stage.   Use the opening to connect with your audience and introduce the scope of your presentation. For instance, in some persuasive talks, you may use the opening moments to explain your position and how it shapes the way you'll be approaching your presentation. Or, perhaps you'll include a modified version of your objective so the audience knows what you plan to accomplish. If you are unknown to anyone in the audience, you may also need to introduce yourself so you can establish some credibility.

"Grab" their attention. Often your audience has other things on their minds or they're not especially interested in your topic. In such cases, use what's known as a "grabber" to get their attention.

- *Consider one of these options:* Some effective grabbers include asking a question, making a promise of what your presentation will deliver, describing a pertinent and vivid image, sharing a startling story or statistic, or using a statement that highlights "what's in it for them" as explained on pages 19–21.

- *Be careful with humor.* Humor can be an effective grabber; however, use it only if it (1) fits your personality and style, (2) is appropriate for every member of the audience, and (3) relates to the topic or occasion. Never use humor that will make anyone feel left out or put down.

Always include a preview. Without a doubt, the most important part of your opening is your preview. The preview provides an outline of what you'll be saying (that is, it tells them what you're going to tell them) and lets them know how long you plan to speak. Because the preview is one of the most important parts of your presentation, it's virtually always included as a carefully designed visual aid. (See pages 105–107 for information about how to design and use a preview visual.)

- *Use a direct structure if possible.* In most presentations, you will state your main conclusions in the opening. In such cases, you are using a direct approach, as we discussed on pages 39–40. Whether you use a direct or indirect approach, you need a preview that is similar to one of these:

  Example preview using the direct approach

  Following the new procedures benefits us in several ways. With the time remaining on the morning schedule, I'll share several of these benefits with you. First, I'll demonstrate how the new guidelines will save you time. Second, I'll point out how they can be used to respond to your clients' billing questions. And finally, I'll explain how they address the major complaint many of you had about the old system.

  Example preview using the indirect approach

  In the next 30 minutes, I want to go over two topics: first, I'll describe the technology problems we're having in the San Francisco and Pittsburgh offices and second, I'll share three options we have in dealing with these challenges.

- *Deliver your preview slowly.* When you deliver your preview, say it deliberately and in conjunction with your preview visual, giving your audience enough time to process it both aurally and visually.

2. Prepare a well-organized body.

As we discussed on pages 40–42, you need to identify the two, three, four, or five "chunks" of information that will form the body of your presentation. If you limit yourself to no more than five sections, your structure will be easy to grasp.

Your idea chart, outline, or storyboard may have already alerted you to an organizational pattern that makes sense for your talk. If not, we'll review some common ordering patterns and explain how to reinforce your structure by using "backward look/forward look" transitions.

Common ways to order an informative presentation: Based on your presentation objective, decide how to chunk the information you've collected so that you can highlight the key points you want to make, emphasize the questions you'll be addressing, review the steps in a process, or compare the alternatives you are presenting. No matter what pattern you select, limit the number of sections you use. For instance, select three, rather than nine, main points. Simplify a six-step process into a three-step one. Or limit the alternatives by combining minor ones into a category of "other options." Here are some examples of possible organizational patterns.

- *Key points:* With this pattern, you select a limited number of points and order them in a sequence that enables you to connect each point to the one that follows. For example, if you wanted to make three key points about your new dividend policy, then your ordering system might look like this: (1) investor attitude moved toward a yield preference, (2) surplus capital rendered the previous payout ratio impractical, (3) tax changes made the new policy more desirable.

- *Key questions:* This pattern groups your content based on questions you'll address with the audience. For instance, you might order a presentation about a business plan with a series of questions: (1) Why is the environment right? (2) What is our competitive advantage? (3) How will we secure start-up funds? (4) Who will lead and manage this venture?

- *Steps in a process:* With this pattern, you use a chronological approach, moving through the steps sequentially. For example, to explain how to sign up for a health-care provider, a speaker may recommend that new employees (1) complete all the medical forms required for employment, (2) review the new "Health Choices" brochure, (3) meet with a benefits counselor to enroll.

- *Alternatives to compare:* With this pattern, you present several alternatives and compare each one to the ones that preceded it. So, if you wanted to compare the desirability of different graduate degrees based on the openings in an organization, you might use this approach: (1) PhDs for senior research positions, (2) MPAs for policy research and grant writing, (3) MBAs for economic research and financial posts, (4) other degrees for non-research positions.

Common ways to order a persuasive presentation: To be persuasive, you need to find an organizational pattern that works best for your situation. If you are using a direct approach (as explained on pages 39–40), you might opt to structure your talk based on your list of recommendations or your product's most important benefits. If you are using an indirect approach, you might use a problem/solutions structure, explaining and recommending your preference as the last solution. You can compare these ordering options by looking at a partial preview statement for each one:

- *List of recommendations (direct approach):* "We can improve our growth and efficiency if we (1) change our product mix and (2) enhance the customer service department."

- *List of benefits (direct approach):* "We should use Ad Graphics as our primary supplier for two reasons: (1) they're able to meet our quality, delivery, and cost requirements, and (2) we'll be making progress on our community relations initiative by using a local printing service."

- *Problem and possible solutions (indirect approach).* "First, I'll describe the technology problems in the San Francisco and Pittsburgh offices. Then, I'll share three alternatives we can consider to deal with these challenges."

Explicit transitions: No matter what type of organizational pattern you choose, you need longer, more explicit transitions between major sections and subsections than you do when you are writing. Listeners do not stay oriented as easily as readers do. They may not even remember what you are listing unless you use clear transitions. So avoid vague transitions, such as "Second . . ." and use explicit ones instead: "The second way to enhance our marketing efforts involves . . ." or "Let's move on to the second marketing recommendation."

"Backward look/forward look" transitions: In addition to more explicit transitions, you also need to use more repetitive ones— because listeners may not remember information they hear only once. The "backward look" refers to recapping the section you just covered, and the "forward look" provides a segue to the upcoming part of your talk.

Although you may feel as if you're being too repetitive, your listeners appreciate these detailed reminders that reinforce your structure—enabling daydreamers to get back on track and alerting attentive listeners that something new is coming up.

Example backward look/forward look:

Now that I've looked at the three elements of the marketing plan **(backward look),** let's turn to the financial implications of that plan **(forward look).**

3. Determine how you'll close.

As the Audience Memory Curve on page 38 shows, your audience is likely to remember your last words. Therefore, your closing should be more than just "thank you" or the all-too-common "no more questions . . . well then, that's it." Although you always want to avoid such "dribble" endings, your closing comments can take many forms. We'll give you a few ideas about how to end and alert you to the challenge of closing your talk after a Q&A session.

To deliver your closing words effectively, pause and breathe before you say them. Once you have finished, wait a few seconds before you head back to your chair. For more insight about how to use your nonverbal behavior to emphasize a message, refer to Chapter 6.

Closing an informative talk: In an information-sharing (or "tell") presentation, use the final moments to recap what you've told them. In most cases, your presentation objective will remind you what is most important and suggest how to close. For example, your last statement may simply be a sound bite from your presentation objective, or it may be a polished version of how you previously described your presentation using the "nutshell" technique, as described on page 56. Just make sure there is some connection between how you close and what you're trying to accomplish.

Closing a persuasive talk: In a persuasive (or "sell") presentation, your closing comments need to close the sale. Use your presentation objective to help you decide how to craft your closing; end in a way that will enable you to measure your presentation's success. For example, you might wrap up by . . .

- *Asking the decision makers* for an order or by requesting authorization to implement your recommendations.
- *Distributing a sign-up sheet* so you can collect the names of people willing to volunteer for your campaign.
- *Restating your most persuasive point* and then arranging to talk privately with the decision maker so you can close the sale during this informal conversation.

Using both initial and final closing statements: If you are planning a Q&A session at the end of your presentation, then you will need two closings. The first one will wrap up your prepared comments and segue into a request for questions. Ideally, the second one will synthesize several pertinent moments from the Q&A session and link them to your presentation objective. If none of the questions can be tied to your presentation objective, then your final closing will be a strong, clear statement that is similar to your initial closing. Always make sure the final words the audience hears are yours and that they are linked to your presentation objective.

SAMPLE INFORMATIVE PRESENTATION	
Opening	Introduction of presenter and topic Main conclusions Preview
Body	Point 1 (followed by a backward look/forward look transition) Point 2 (followed by a backward look/forward look transition) Point 3 (followed by a backward look and segue to closing)
Closing	Summary of points/concluding statement

SAMPLE PERSUASIVE PRESENTATION (FOLLOWED BY Q&A SESSION)	
Opening	Introduction of presenter and topic Recommendation Preview
Body	Benefit 1 (followed by a backward look/forward look transition) Benefit 2 (followed by a backward look/forward look transition) Benefit 3 (followed by a backward look and segue to closing)
Closing	Initial closing (including a request for questions) Q&A session Final closing (featuring a call for action)

III. PREPARE FOR Q&A.

Most presentations involve interaction between the speaker and audience in the form of Q&A.

I. Get ready for their questions.

Consider the audience's Q&A expectations and their possible questions.

Decide when to take questions.   You have two options about when to take questions; compare their advantages and drawbacks.

- *Holding questions for the end:* The main advantage of ending with questions is that you maintain control of the schedule and flow of information. However, there are risks with this choice: (1) you may confuse people if they can't ask their questions as they occur, and (2) you could place yourself in an awkward position if people ask questions after you've asked them not to do so.

- *Taking questions throughout:* If you take questions during the presentation, the questions will be more meaningful to the questioner, the responses will be immediate, and your audience may listen more attentively. However, questions during the presentation can upset your schedule and waste time if you go off on tangents. To alleviate these problems: (1) budget some time for questions rather than planning to talk during the entire time you've been allotted; (2) consider making extra visuals so you can explore some topics in detail if you have time or are asked, but can skip the extra material if time runs short; (3) control digressions by using the effective listening and responding skills described on the following pages.

Expect and value questions.   Try not to get defensive when someone adds a comment or asks a question. Think of it as a compliment—"my audience is interested enough to seek clarification or justification"—or as a useful bit of information—"now I know how the decision maker is reacting to my recommendation."

Prepare to answer questions.   If you anticipate questions, you will be better able to address and even welcome them. Consider asking someone to play "devil's advocate" during your rehearsal. Have this person pose common questions—those related to value, cost, alternatives, action steps, details, obstacles, risk, and timing—and then challenge you with more unexpected and difficult questions, too.

2. Refine your listening skills.

Listening expert Robert Bolton breaks listening skills into three clusters of behavior. Use these skills to (1) look like a good listener, (2) encourage participation, and (3) paraphrase the questions you are asked.

Look like a good listener.   Use various nonverbal behaviors to show your audience you are interested in their questions. Check your posture, movement, and eye contact to make sure you appear attentive. Also make sure the atmosphere is right for Q&A.

- *Maintain a posture of involvement.* Face the questioner directly. Keep your arms and hands out of the way.
- *Hold your body still.* Avoid distracting movements, such as tapping your feet, clicking a pen, or fidgeting with your notes. Let your body language signal that you're listening intently.
- *Make eye contact.* Look at the questioner, observing his or her whole face so that you can pick up nonverbal cues.
- *Create an environment suitable for listening.* If appropriate, consider moving to the side of the podium or in front of a table, closing the distance between you and the audience. During Q&A, turn up the lights so the audience can be the focus of your attention.

Encourage participation.   Get people to participate by posing open-ended questions, being silent, and using small signals that encourage them to continue talking.

- *Open the door for questions.* Use open-ended questions that can't just be answered "yes" or "no." Rather than begin with the words "Can you . . ." or "Do you . . ." start with phrases such as "What's your view of . . ." or "Tell me about . . ."
- *Be silent: don't interrupt.* After you've asked a question or invited people to participate in a Q&A session, give them time to think. Wait patiently. Give them at least 10 to 15 seconds to collect their thoughts. Don't say anything while you wait. Also, be silent as you listen to their questions. If you interrupt, you won't hear the entire question, and you'll send a signal that you're rushing them.
- *Use minimal encouragers.* Also consider using little cues, called "minimal encouragers," which entice a speaker to continue: nodding, smiling, tilting your head, widening your eyes, or saying "uh huh." As long as these signals are natural, they communicate that you are genuinely interested in listening to the question.

Paraphrase the question. A paraphrase is a brief statement that captures the essence of the question that was asked. It involves more than just repeating the question. Unlike the paraphrasing used in active listening, Q&A paraphrasing can be used to alter the tone or direction of an interaction, giving the presenter more control. Use this tool to (1) make sure that everyone stays involved, (2) clarify the question being asked, (3) respond to emotional as well as factual content, and (4) diffuse difficult questions. Paraphrasing is particularly important in these instances:

- *When the question is hard to hear:* If someone sitting in the front row asks a question, those sitting in the back may not be able to hear it. Therefore, you should either repeat or paraphrase the question so everyone knows what was asked. In addition, be sure to paraphrase the question if the questioner's accent is unfamiliar to the audience.

- *When the feelings trump the facts:* Questioners' vocal tone and facial expression sometimes express more information than their actual words. In such cases, you'll want to paraphrase the feelings as well as the words, perhaps saying something like this: "I recognize that many of you are frustrated by the new paperwork requirements, so let's get to the root of Juan's question: Why do we need to replace a simple, one-page form with this new detailed one?"

- *When the question is difficult to answer:* Questions can be tough to answer for many different reasons, ranging from the structure of the question to the hostility of the questioner. For an overview of the various types of difficult questions, see pages 71–75. Such questions always need to be paraphrased before you respond.

- *When you need time to think:* Paraphrasing gives you a moment to collect your thoughts, which means that you can listen to the whole question rather than form your answer before the questioner has finished.

3. Respond effectively.

Effective responses help you accomplish your objective. Ideally, they should also be interesting and delivered in a way that keeps your audience involved.

Stay on message.   When you are asked a question, think of it as a chance to make your message heard. To do so, use two powerful techniques: "bridging" and "flagging."

- *Bridging* connects your response to something that is part of your presentation objective. A bridge can be a connecting phrase, such as "which means. . . ," or a simple word, such as "and." For example, a bridge might sound like this: "Claire, you've asked an important question about wildlife safety, so I'll address the potential hazards you mentioned *and* explain how we protect birds, animals and plant life at our facilities."

- *Flagging* draws attention to your most salient point. Typical flags include phrases such as: "What's at stake here is . . ." or "The critical point is . . ."

Balance brevity with interesting detail.   Ideally, your responses will be noteworthy and memorable. You will also want many of them to be brief so you can maintain the interactive nature of Q&A.

- *Make your responses interesting.* Vivid words and well-crafted sound bites are interesting; rambling explanations are not. Stories told in the present tense can bring listeners into the moment; those that plod along chronologically often fall flat.

- *Either use brief responses or well-structured longer ones.* If people's hands go up before you finish, either your comments aren't brief enough or you are not clearly wrapping them up. While brief replies hold people's interest, sometimes a question will require a longer, more detailed explanation. In such cases, begin with an overview that gives the audience an idea of how you plan to reply and end by using your vocal traits to signal that you are done.

Keep everyone involved.   Paraphrasing the hard-to-hear questions is one way to keep everyone aware of what's being discussed. In addition, call on people from various parts of the room, perhaps alternating from one section of the audience to another as you take questions. When speaking to those in the front, use enough volume so people in the back can hear. And don't just look at the questioner when you respond; focus on other audience members, too.

4. Listen for challenging questions.

Tough questions come in all shapes and sizes, but they tend to fall into three categories: (1) unclear questions, (2) questions framed in a limiting way, (3) and questions for which you don't know the answer.

Unclear questions: Perhaps you've used your best listening skills, but you still have no idea what you've been asked. When a question is unclear use an "I" response rather than a "you" response. In other words, say "I'm not sure I understand the question" rather than "Your question is confusing." Sometimes the question is only a bit unclear. At such times, paraphrase to check that your assumptions are correct. In addition, be aware of three common types of unclear questions:

- *Vague questions* use nonspecific language. When you hear words such as "it," "this," "that notion," or "the other option," try to clarify your understanding of the vague words with a paraphrase.

- *Long multi-questions* string three, four, or even more questions together. Based on the situation and the questioner, you have several options in dealing with multi-questions: (1) synthesize all the questions and offer a single response; (2) start with the question you like best, avoiding the ones you don't want to address; and (3) answer one part of the question and ask the questioner to remind you of the remaining questions.

- *Broad questions* inquire about wide-ranging issues that could never be addressed in a limited time. To deal with them, either narrow the focus and respond to the question or point out the broad nature of the question and offer to address it later, perhaps after the presentation.

Limiting questions: Many types of questions seem to limit your options or lead you toward a response that you don't want to give. They include forced-choice, hypothetical, empty-chair, loaded-language, and false-premise questions. In addition, listen for distorted paraphrases that mischaracterize what you have said.

- *Forced-choice* questions imply there are a limited number of options and ask you to choose one. Often they use the word *or.* For example, "What's more important, the amount of time a doctor can spend with each patient *or* the number of patients that can be seen each day?" Remember that "both" choices can be important. Other forced-choice structures ask you to rank items on the questioner's scale or to identify what's "most" significant. Once again, you can reframe the questions so you are setting the parameters.

- *Hypothetical* questions create a situation that doesn't exist, although it could be a potential reality. "If the FDA rejects your application, how will it affect other drugs in your research pipeline?" In such cases, it's best to stick with what is known rather than focus on what might occur. If the questioner is your boss, then you'll likely have to accept the premise; if the questioner is a reporter, then do not speculate.

- *Empty-chair* questions ask you to comment on something said by a third party, someone not in the room. If you didn't hear the CEO's comments or you haven't read the statement put out by the Attorney General, don't even begin to evaluate what was supposedly said or why it was said.

- *Loaded-language* questions include colorful words, phrases, and perhaps even sarcasm that make the question a minefield. Neutralize the language by using a paraphrase. Don't say: "I am not a heartless bureaucrat," say: "I know you're disappointed. I wish we had more resources so we could help everyone on the waiting list."

- *False-premise* questions begin with an incorrect assumption: "When did the accounting department begin falsifying their reports?" To respond, correct the assumption: "If you're concerned with the accuracy of our financial reports, let me assure you that we have open books and all our accounting practices are carefully monitored; we stand by our numbers."

- *Distorted paraphrases* aren't really questions; they are inaccurate summaries of your comments. For example, suppose you just finished explaining how your staffing levels would hold steady and someone distorts your remarks by saying: "So you're telling us layoffs are inevitable." Don't ignore these remarks. Correct them by saying, "Let me clarify: our staffing levels will be the same next year as they are this year."

"Don't know" questions: If you don't know the answer, don't bluff. Instead say, "I don't know." Or better, suggest where the person can find the answer. Or better yet, offer to get the answer yourself— "Off the top of my head, I don't know the demographics for that region, but I can easily get that information for you by tomorrow morning." Then be sure you follow up.

In other cases, you may just need a little time to gather your thoughts. If so, here are a few stalling options: (1) repeat or paraphrase the question, (2) turn the question outward by asking the questioner or the entire audience for their ideas and opinions, (3) take a moment to reflect by saying something such as "Karla, let me think about your question for a second," or (4) write the question on a board or flip chart so that you can discuss it as a group.

5. Control difficult or hostile audience members.

Occasionally, audience members don't have your best interest at heart. They may try to take control of the discussion, attack you or your ideas, or distract you in some way. If so, you need to control the situation without letting the confrontation get personal. Here are some techniques to handle hostility.

Types of difficult questioners and audience members: Different behaviors annoy different people, which means we can't possibly list all the ways audience members can be difficult. Nevertheless, here are a few of the troublesome types and how you might handle them:

- *Pontificators* enjoy the sound of their voices. They ramble on and on, sometimes never even asking a question. To respond, listen intently so you can paraphrase something of value and then bridge to a message that gets you back on track.

- *Nitpickers* focus on minutia and take you off message. You can acknowledge that "yes, the actual figure is 14.89 percent" and then explain that you would like to focus on trends rather than on specific data points during your talk.

- *Needlers* use sarcasm or try to belittle you in some way. Don't mimic their sarcastic tone or try to embarrass them. Just restate your opinions calmly and clearly, using logical reasoning to back your views.

- *Distracters* initiate side conversations, roll their eyes, or mumble disapprovingly under their breath. You can move toward people having side conversations or pointedly wait until they stop talking, but don't become overly confrontational. Focus on the people who are interested instead.

General tips for handling a hostile audience member: How you manage the interaction between you and a hostile questioner will depend on many variables. For instance, you would deal differently with a hostile boss than you would a nasty colleague. Yet, in all cases, you want to maintain your credibility by being polite, trying to find points of mutual agreement, using effective listening skills, and connecting with the audience members who are willing to be fair.

- *Be polite,* even to the rudest audience members. For example, don't snap at a pontificator by saying "So, what exactly is your point?" Of all the tips for handling difficult audiences, being polite is the most important.

- *Lessen hostility* by pointing to common ground, in essence agreeing to disagree. For example, say something like "We don't seem to agree on how to handle this customer service problem, but since we agree that we want to do what's best for our customers, we can begin by conducting an assessment of their needs and views."

- *Paraphrase the feelings behind the question.* If the nonverbal behavior implies that there's more to the message than the words alone indicate, acknowledge the questioner's emotions in your paraphrase by noting the anger or frustration.

- *Stop repeat offenders tactfully,* perhaps by putting up your hand and saying "I'm sorry to interrupt, but I want to make sure we end on time, so let me touch on the issue you mentioned by saying . . ."

- *Look elsewhere afterwards.* After responding, do not direct your eye contact toward the difficult questioner. If you do, you're just inviting this person to make another challenging comment. Instead, look at the friendly faces so you can avoid repeated volleys with the troublemaker. Also be sure to look at supportive faces when you finish your talk; you don't want to invite another outburst during your closing.

Differences based on interpersonal style: Communication expert Joann Baney suggests that you analyze your own interpersonal style to get some ideas about how you are likely to fare in a hostile Q&A environment. In *Guide to Interpersonal Skills* (cited in the bibliography on page 136), she differentiates between two types of assertiveness: a telling style and an asking style. Knowing your tendencies will help you determine how to respond to hostile questioners.

- *A telling style is direct.* People with this preference are talkative. They tend to use above-average volume and forceful or large gestures. In addition, they don't shy away from conflict. When engaged in hostile exchanges, they can become (1) autocratic, barking orders to people in the room or (2) challenging, using their quick wit to launch verbal grenades at difficult audience members.

   If you have a telling style, don't label a situation "hostile" too quickly. Be careful not to interrupt, yell, or point at the hostile audience member. Remember, as soon as you verbally attack someone in the audience, you usually lose credibility. Once your credibility is lost, it's hard to get it back.

- *An asking style is less direct* Someone with this preference tends to talk less and make fewer direct requests than someone with a telling style. In addition, an asking style is characterized by lower-than-average volume, a tendency to listen intently, and a desire to avoid conflict.

  If your style is more "asking" than "telling," don't hold yourself back, waiting to make sure someone is truly being difficult; by the time you have made this judgment, the audience has likely made the same determination. Therefore, once you sense hostility, immediately use techniques to help you disengage from the troublemaker, such as holding up a hand to stop a pontificator. Force yourself to correct anyone who incorrectly paraphrases your comments. And remember to keep your volume loud enough so you aren't drowned out by the hostile people in the audience.

If you used both strategic and topical information to structure your content and prepare for questions, you should now have an effective opening, body, and closing for your presentation. You should also have a good idea about the questions the audience will ask. Next, we will turn to designing your visual aids.

CHAPTER 5 OUTLINE

I. DECIDE ON THE TYPE OF VISUAL AID.
1. Factors to consider
2. Common options

II. BEGIN WITH YOUR MESSAGE TITLES.
1. Identify your important messages.
2. Turn topic titles into message titles.

III. THINK VISUALLY AS YOU DESIGN.
1. Use data-driven charts to illustrate your numbers.
2. Use diagrams to clarify concepts.
3. Use color systematically.
4. Highlight with spot color and animation.
5. Add variety with other visual elements.

IV. USE READABLE AND SIMPLE LAYOUTS.
1. Use readable lettering.
2. Watch for wordiness.
3. Delete chartjunk.

V. BE CONSISTENT AND CORRECT.
1. Design your own template.
2. Provide structural consistency.
3. Check every visual.

CHAPTER 5

Design the Visuals

After you have decided what to say, you can focus on your visual aids. If designed and used properly, visual aids make your ideas clearer and more memorable because the combination of seeing plus hearing is more effective than just seeing or hearing alone.

As you design your visual aids, we suggest that you (1) choose the most effective type of visual, (2) begin with your titles so you can control which important messages the audience will see, (3) "think visually" so you will design slides and pages that are more than just bullet lists, (4) use readable and simple layouts so your visuals are easy to see and use, and (5) ensure consistent and correct results so that you, rather than an ineffective visual aid, will be the focus of your presentation.

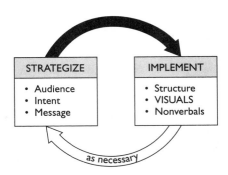

I. DECIDE ON THE TYPE OF VISUAL AID.

Before you begin designing your visual aids, think about the equipment you plan to use.

I. Factors to consider

Consider your constraints and resources, basing your decision on the audience, your expertise, the location, and other issues associated with the various options.

The audience: Your audience may have expectations about the type of visuals you should use. Some may be linked to cultural norms, and some may be a result of the size of the group.

- *Using what the audience expects:* Find out what is standard for the organization or culture. Some high-tech groups would consider an overhead projector as outdated as a black-and-white TV. Some government and community organizations would consider glossy, four-color handouts inappropriate, given their budget constraints. And some environmentally concerned groups might prefer that you limit your use of paper, using only recycled materials and two-sided printing if you must use handouts.

- *Going against visual aid norms:* If you are the only presenter on the day's agenda not using PowerPoint, then your presentation will stand out from the rest. As you may recall, doing something different is a way to get attention. Just make sure an atypical choice is appropriate for the situation.

- *Factoring in the size of the group:* (1) If the audience is large, the standard choices are projected visuals or presentation decks. Options such as whiteboards may not be visible if people are sitting far way. (2) With smaller audiences, you can still use a slide show or play a video clip, but you may want to project them on a small monitor rather than a gigantic screen. Presentation decks also work with small groups as do informal options, such as boards and flip charts.

- *Factoring in the formality of the situation:* Handwritten visuals are less formal than those generated by a computer. If you want to include interaction or discussion as part of your talk, then using a flip chart or whiteboard will seem less scripted and signal that you want to include ideas from the audience.

Your expertise: In general, if something is new, you will need time, and perhaps some assistance, to master it.

- *What equipment can you use with confidence?* Since your nonverbal delivery is affected by your visuals, it's often best to choose something you have used successfully before. If you want to try something new, allow extra time for preparation and practice. For tips on how to use various types of visual aids, see pages 125–127.
- *How much assistance is available?* If possible, try something new only when you have expert assistance. For instance, if you have never tried to set up a videoconference, arrange to have an audiovisual (AV) person in the room to assist you. Similarly, if you are using PowerPoint, Flash, or some other type of software for the first time, get help from someone who can show you how to use it wisely.

The location: The place you are presenting will influence your choices. If you haven't seen the location, be sure you ask about the room's dimensions, furniture layout, screen, lighting, and type of equipment that is available.

- *Room size and furniture layout:* Large rooms with tiers of fixed seating, stages, and built-in podiums influence your choice of visuals, restrict where you can place them, and sometimes require that you use a microphone. Visuals that rely on handwritten text tend to work best in small rooms, but small rooms can also pose visual aid challenges. For instance, even a moderately sized conference room may not be able to accommodate bulky projection equipment or a large, portable whiteboard. Some small rooms don't even have enough space for a flip chart.
- *Screen size:* The size of a projected image affects the readability of your visuals. For example, according to visual aid master, Gene Zelazny, a 20-point font will be visible from 45 feet away if the screen image is 12 feet wide; the same text will only be visible from 30 feet away if the screen image is 6 feet wide.
- *Lighting issues:* Find out about the lighting, including window placement and dimming options. It's fine to turn out the lights to show a video clip, but try to keep most of the lights on during your talk. Audiences tend to get very sleepy when they sit in the dark.
- *Equipment availability:* Some rooms are equipped with built-in projection and wireless internet access; others are not. Find out what's already in the room and what can be brought in. Don't just assume you'll have what you'll need.

2. Common options

Visual aid equipment falls into four major categories: (1) multimedia, (2) still projections, (3) boards and flip charts, and (4) hard copy. This section describes them and notes some of the challenges of using them successfully.

Multimedia: These high-tech options enable you to project images and sounds from a computer, the internet, video, DVD, and audio sound systems. If using a system for the first time, arrive early and work with an AV person. Also bring handouts so you will have a backup in case the equipment malfunctions.

- *Installed projection systems:* The image quality of these systems varies, partially because they use different technologies, such as liquid crystal display (LCD), plasma, or cathode ray tube (CRT), which has the best resolution. If you are using a system for the first time, arrive early enough to check font size, colors, and problems with animation. Presenting from your own laptop helps avoid some compatibility glitches.

- *Portable projectors:* Most likely, the color you see on your laptop won't match what gets projected. Leave enough time to make color adjustments.

Still projection: These systems include 35 mm slide projectors, overhead projectors, and the more recent document cameras.

- *35 mm slides:* Although used less and less, these slides have exceptionally high resolution. Nevertheless, they require darkened rooms and are time consuming and costly to produce when compared to the more typical PowerPoint slides.

- *Overhead projectors:* These projectors require special acetate sheets and pens, but they are versatile since you can write on them as you can with a flip chart. You can also prepare them ahead of time. Nevertheless, the technology is now "old fashioned," and the projectors have large arms that often block the view of some audience members.

- *Document cameras:* With these projectors, you can project printed pages, images, or objects. Although they have less effective resolution than overheads or slides, they are frequently used for videoconferencing.

Boards and flip charts: If used well, both boards and flip charts can enhance discussions, partially because you can use them in a well-lit room. In some cases, titles or other elements can be prepared ahead, but typically presenters write on these visuals during the presentation, which can be a challenge for people with poor handwriting. All have limited room for text and images; therefore, you'll need to erase the board or flip the page to generate more space. They are less formal than projected visuals.

- *Traditional boards:* These include whiteboards that need special markers and old-fashioned blackboards that use chalk. They don't leave a permanent record.

- *Electronic copy boards:* These boards provide a hard copy of what's written on them and can even be viewed on computer screens in multiple locations.

- *"Live" boards:* These boards have an additional feature; they can be annotated online in multiple locations.

- *Flip charts:* Although they can be large and clumsy to transport, flip charts are versatile, and the pages can be saved for future reference or can be posted on walls to stimulate discussions.

Hard copy: Sometimes it's important for the audience to have a hard copy of some or all of what's mentioned during the presentation. These printed pages can be distributed before, during, or after your talk. If the audience has them during the talk, they can be used for note taking; however, audience members often skip ahead, which makes it hard to keep them focused on what you're saying.

- *Decks* are also known as "pitch-books" or "flip books." This type of visual can be used as a primary visual aid or as a backup for a high-tech option. Decks range from professionally printed pages with wire binding to black-and-white printouts, stapled in the corner. It's easier for audience members to use decks if they have tables or desks in front of them. In all cases, be sure you number the pages in your deck so you can refer your audience to the right spot.

- *Handouts* can provide detailed information to augment your visual aids. For example, you may use a handout to show a complex diagram or table of data too detailed for projection. Other handouts are copies of your PowerPoint slides, perhaps printed with two, three, or four images per page. Common take-away handouts include reading lists, company brochures, and reprinted articles that may be of interest to the audience.

II. BEGIN WITH YOUR MESSAGE TITLES.

Don't make your titles an afterthought. Instead, once you have selected the type of visual you plan to use, but before you start to design, think about your titles. Identify your important messages so you can control what the audience hears and sees.

Rather than using titles that are merely vague words or phrases, learn how to create message titles—statements that help you inform or persuade your audience. Message titles are descriptive. They use carefully constructed messages that speed information sharing and influence visual aid design.

1. Identify your important messages.

Often, people make too many visuals; some try to project 30 slides in a 20-minute talk. As a result, they either get through only a small part of their presentation or rush through their visuals, barely allowing the audience to take in one image before moving to the next. In most cases, these presenters didn't identify their important messages; instead, they tried to highlight too much material or designed visual aids to double as their notes.

Not everything you plan to say can or should appear on a visual. Instead, use your visuals to (1) reinforce the structure of your talk, (2) emphasize your main messages, and (3) draw attention to important supporting points.

Reinforce the structure.   Typically, you will use visuals to introduce the opening of your talk, highlight the various sections of your presentation, and emphasize your recommendations or conclusions.

- *Title visual:* The first image seen by the audience is your title slide, the cover of your deck, or your first flip chart page. Highlight your name and the title of your talk so audience members know they are in the right place and see your name before you begin.

- *Preview visual:* Other visuals might be used in the opening, but the one that reinforces your structure is the preview visual. The preview visual may take the form of a "table of contents" in your deck or be the list of topics you plan to cover, handwritten on a flip chart. It might also be the preview slide in your slide show. For more information about how to design and use your preview visual, see pages 105–107.

- *Section visuals:* In long PowerPoint shows, you may want to project your preview slide more than once, perhaps using dimmed text or another highlighting technique to show the transition from one section to the next. Similarly, in long deck presentations, you may want to insert section dividers and trackers to visually emphasize the structure of your talk. Sometimes trackers are also included in slide shows. See page 106 for examples of trackers and for more information about how to use them.

- *Conclusion (or recommendation) visuals:* Whether you show your conclusions or recommendations during the opening or closing (or both), these messages are good choices for visual reinforcement.

Emphasize your main messages.   Some visual aid options allow for more visual images than others. For instance, if you are using a whiteboard, you will need time to create the visual and then erase it before you add another image. Nevertheless, even if you are using a slide show, you can't make everything stand out. So here are a few ways to separate your main messages from the less important ideas:

- *Remember your objective.* Your presentation objective may provide clues about what needs to be seen as well as heard. For instance, if your presentation objective identifies a message you want the audience to hear, such as a sound bite, you may want to turn this message into a title for one of your visual aids.

- *Recall the nutshell technique.* If you used the nutshell technique described on page 56, then you may find an important message embedded in this summary. Decide whether part of the nutshell message can and should be turned into a title.

- *Try a storyboard.* If you ordered your ideas using a storyboard, as discussed on page 57, then you've already identified some of the images that need to be seen as well as heard. If you used a different technique to order your ideas, then you can use your outline or idea chart as a springboard for doing a storyboard.

Draw attention to important supporting points.   Most of your main messages are probably backed by compelling evidence. These supporting points might rely on quantitative data, examples, or benefit statements that explain "what's in it for them." To find the important secondary messages, look at your outline, idea chart, or storyboard and examine the ideas that you consider backup points. Be selective. Decide (1) which points provide the strongest support and (2) which will make the most powerful visuals.

2. Turn topic titles into message titles.

Unfortunately, many visual aids use "topic titles." Topic titles note the subject being discussed, but don't tell the audience what point to take away. "Message titles," on the other hand, clarify your point, speed up information sharing, enable your visuals to make "stand-alone sense," and influence visual aid design.

Message titles clarify your point.   Look at the column charts below. The first one uses the topic title "Sales Results." It lets the audience decide what point the image is making. The second chart shows the same data, but this version uses a message title. It tells the audience exactly what you want them to see. That same chart could have had many other message titles, such as: (1) sales are increasing, (2) sales more than doubled in the second quarter, (3) sales held steady from April through September, (4) sales in the first quarter were exceptionally low, and so on. Notice that each of the message titles includes a verb, as do most message titles.

Example: ineffective topic title   *Example: effective message title*

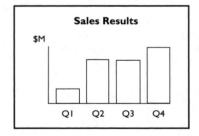   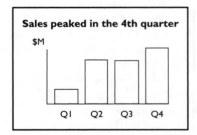

Although message titles are especially important when showing quantitative data, they are also beneficial when using diagrams and bullet lists. In tell and sell situations—times when you want to control the message—these titles clarify your points. Nevertheless, there may be times when you want the audience to discuss a visual; in such cases, using a topic title would prevent you from influencing their views.

Message titles speed up information sharing. If you include a message title, your audience won't need as much time to examine the rest of the slide or deck page. In addition, using message titles enables you to streamline your bullet lists; you won't need to include as much text if the title frames the supporting points. Message titles even help you transition gracefully from one visual to the next. By contrast, topic titles usually take longer to introduce.

While they accelerate comprehension, ironically, message titles tend to be longer than topic titles. If you examine the following table, you will discover that the topic titles lack the verbs and details that are part of the message titles.

FROM TOPIC TITLE TO MESSAGE TITLE	
Ineffective topic title . . .	. . . transformed into a longer, but clearer, message title
Agenda: Bard Company	Increase growth and efficiency at Bard
Web Traffic in August	Web traffic dropped off in August
Budget Allocation	20% of the budget went to overtime
Results	Air quality was the top concern
Experience vs. Sales	Experienced brokers sold more bonds

Message titles help create "stand-alone sense." The words and images on your visuals should make sense, on their own, to someone seeing them for the first time. Achieving this stand-alone sense is easier if you use a message title.

- *Help viewers follow along:* Message titles broadcast the main point, which helps latecomers understand the context of what they're hearing as they walk in the room. These titles also allow daydreamers to reconnect to the current focus of your presentation.

- *Provide useful records:* Visuals that make stand-alone sense are especially useful after the presentation. Whether people are reviewing an email file of your PowerPoint slides or flipping though your deck, your message titles will help them make sense out of what they see on each slide or page. For more information about stand-alone sense, see page 102.

Message titles influence your design decisions. If you are using a large flip chart, a whiteboard, a deck, or slides, you should have plenty of room for message titles—if you plan for them. For instance, when you design PowerPoint slides, leave two lines for your titles when you create a template (as discussed on pages 104–107). And when creating data-driven charts, use your message title to determine whether to choose a pie, bar, column, or some other type of chart.

- *Influence overall PowerPoint design:* With slides, select a standard title size (usually 28- to 36-point) and then edit your titles to fit on two lines. When titles wrap to a second line, they usually look better if they are left-justified rather than centered. With a deck, you will use much smaller title fonts. Whether designing slides or deck pages, make the titles distinct from the other text. To create this distinction, you can: (1) use a visibly smaller font for the regular text, (2) make the title bold, (3) use different colors for the title and other text, as long as both choices are highly visible, or (4) add a line between the title and the text or use a different colored background for the title and text areas. See page 98 for tips on font selection and pages 92–94 for more information about using color.

- *Determine which comparison to use:* You can't figure out what type of chart to create if you haven't identified the message in your data. In every spreadsheet, you will have dozens of possible messages that make all sorts of different comparisons. Some of these messages might show how numbers have changed over time, while others may break down a unit into proportions or shares. As shown below, four of the message titles from the previous page imply different types of data comparisons. On pages 87–89, we explain how to choose the right chart for each of the following comparisons:

FROM MESSAGE TITLES TO COMPARISONS	
Title	**Comparison**
Web traffic dropped off in August	Time series
20% of budget went to overtime	Component
Air quality was the top concern	Item
Experienced brokers sold more bonds	Correlation

III. THINK VISUALLY AS YOU DESIGN.

In this section, we will share some ideas about how to go beyond lists and tables so your visual aids are actually "visual."

1. Use data-driven charts to illustrate your numbers.

As we already mentioned, every numerical table offers scores of potential messages. As the presenter, it's your job to locate these messages, decide which ones are relevant, and turn the corresponding numbers into easy-to-comprehend charts. To do so, we continue to follow Gene Zelazny's method from *Say It With Charts*: determine your message, identify the comparison, and then select the chart form. Using this approach, we'll examine common data comparisons and point out the chart forms appropriate for each one.

Time series (changes over time):   These comparisons use time as a variable, plotted on the x-axis. A time-series comparison can show a change that spans seconds, days, quarters, or decades. It can focus on increases, decreases, seasonal fluctuations, or a significant upturn. If your message is about a pattern occurring over time, then you have three basic chart options: column, line, or area charts.

- *Choose column charts for limited data points* and for times when you want to emphasize specific numbers as much as the trend. To make your column chart more visual, increase the width of the columns and reduce the space between them. Also get rid of "chartjunk" as shown on page 103.

- *Use line charts to emphasize trends.* When you have many data points, a line chart will show the trend more elegantly than columns. Unfortunately, the PowerPoint's default settings use thin lines and needless data markers. Therefore, increase the width of the trend line and eliminate the distracting data markers, tick marks, and grid lines. Always delete the legend and label the lines instead. When projecting a line chart, limit the number of trend lines on your chart; more than three will be hard to differentiate.

- *Select area charts for showing a single trend.* If you are designing a line chart with a single trend line, consider switching to an area chart. Because it shades the entire area under the line, an area chart is far more visual.

Item (ranking or variation among items):   An item comparison ranks items, such as companies, products, and so on. With an item comparison, the message isn't about time. It's about how certain items are similar or which one ranks first, third, or even last. A message that indicates an item comparison could be "Plant A produced fewer gizmos than two other plants." For such comparisons, use a simple bar chart. Bar charts are easy to label because you can insert the label beside or even on the bar.

Component (parts of a whole):   A component comparison shows the relationship among parts of a whole. Your message might be about percentages, shares, or proportions. For components of one item, choose a pie chart; for components of multiple items, you will probably select another option.

- *Choose pie charts for simple comparisons.* Pie charts are easy to make, which may explain why they are sometimes overused. If you are projecting a pie chart, limit the number of slices; more than six will be difficult to differentiate and label. If you are featuring one slice, put it at the "12 o'clock" position of the pie. In all cases, eliminate the legend and label your pie slices as we did on page 103.

- *Consider other choices for multiple component comparisons.* If the message is about how one budget component changes over time, then use subdivided columns, with a y-axis that goes from 0 to 100%. If the message isn't linked to time, then consider subdivided bars, with an x-axis that goes from 0 to 100%.

Correlation (pattern between variables):   These comparisons show the relationship—or lack of relationship—between two variables. For example, perhaps you want to show that the most expensive canned foods received the highest taste-test ratings. To show the pattern between price and ratings, you could choose a dot chart or paired bars, depending on how many food items were in the data pool.

- *Try dot charts when you have many data points.* If you were plotting the price and ratings for 20 items, then your best option would be to plot each point with a dot and insert a line to show the pattern.

- *Use paired bars for limited data points.* If comparing the price and ratings for four items, then use paired bars, as shown on page 89.

- *Be careful with complex correlation comparisons.* Be especially careful with bubble charts, which are dot charts with an extra dimension: the size of the dot. These charts, which are popular with consultants and marketing executives, need to be built gradually and explained carefully.

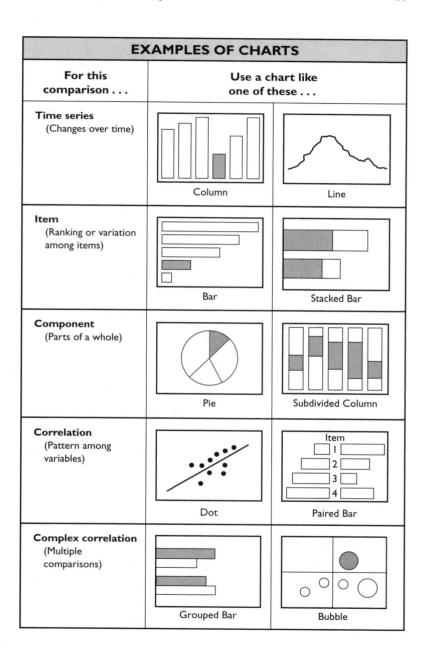

EXAMPLES OF CHARTS

For this comparison . . .	Use a chart like one of these . . .	
Time series (Changes over time)	Column	Line
Item (Ranking or variation among items)	Bar	Stacked Bar
Component (Parts of a whole)	Pie	Subdivided Column
Correlation (Pattern among variables)	Dot	Paired Bar
Complex correlation (Multiple comparisons)	Grouped Bar	Bubble

2. Use diagrams to clarify concepts.

Just as data-driven charts help your audience see "how much," concept diagrams help them see "how," "when," or "which one." These diagrams simplify complex ideas. They also add interest, providing a respite from overused bullet lists. Although used for many purposes, concept diagrams are especially useful for illustrating relationships and indicating flow. Arrows, lines, and shapes are the building blocks of such diagrams, but these elements can also be used to add emphasis to other types of charts.

Some diagrams illustrate relationships.   They can show how elements interact, parts overlap, items connect, segments relate, and components compare. Here are just a few of the ways you can use them to depict relationships:

- *To show interaction,* use connected shapes, like a Venn diagram, which implies overlap. Make one concept part of a larger framework by putting one shape inside another. Show a connection among items by placing them along a shape's perimeter, adding arrows as we did on page 2.
- *To emphasize structure,* use an idea chart similar to the one on page 58. If several secondary concepts are linked to one major idea, try a radial or honeycomb layout like the one on page 91. If concepts build off a foundation, consider using a pyramid diagram.
- *To compare concepts,* use a T-chart or two distinct shapes, such as two boxes. For more complex interactions between variables, use a matrix. To compare the elements of three or more ideas, consider using a simple table.

Other diagrams highlight sequence.   Among other things, diagrams can show the steps in a process, the order of events, and the repetition of stages. Use them to show the following:

- *Linear flow:* Arrows, chevrons, and lines imply movement. The diagram on page 95 shows a chevron that could be used to review the steps in a process.
- *Time sequence:* Time lines illustrate events over time. Gantt charts are a type of time line. As shown on page 91, they position bars over a time line to show the starting and stopping point for various stages of a long-term project.
- *Circular flow:* When flow isn't linear, curved arrows or shapes connected by arrows or lines can show a cyclical pattern or stages that repeat.

EXAMPLES OF DIAGRAMS

To show . . .	. . . use a diagram like one of these:	
Interaction	Venn Diagram	Arrow and Shapes
Structure	Pyramid Diagram	Honeycomb Diagram
Comparison	T-Chart	Matrix
Linear flow	Chevron	Gantt Chart
Circular flow	Cycle	Stages in a Cycle

3. Use color systematically.

Color is another visual element available, in some form, with most visual aid options. Selecting colors is especially challenging when you have thousands of options—as you do with PowerPoint. In these cases, select a simple palette of colors and use them in a consistent way on all your visuals. Keeping the audience in mind, choose combinations that are highly visible and aesthetically pleasing. Whether you are printing or projecting these colors, always test your choices; what you see on your computer won't be the same as what gets printed or projected.

Keep your palette simple.   For most slides or deck pages, limit your palette to three colors in addition to black, gray, and white. Avoid what graphic artist Jan White calls "the fruit salad effect"—a jumble of colors that look pretty but don't make anything stand out.

- *For projected slides:* You can use a dark background—for instance black, navy blue, or dark green—and two or three lighter colors for text and graphics. Or you can choose a light background like cream or beige, using several darker colors for the lettering. Sometimes white backgrounds aren't the best choice because they can cause an annoying glare.

- *For color printouts:* White is a great background choice for printed pages. With a white page, you can use a palette of darker colors like black, royal blue, gray-blue, and maroon. Be cautious with dark backgrounds for the following reasons: (1) printing colored backgrounds uses lots of toner, making decks expensive to produce; (2) using dark backgrounds often results in streaky or faded-looking colors; (3) matching printed color to projected color is very difficult: computers mix the primary colors of light (blue, green, and red), while printers mix toner colors (yellow, magenta, and cyan) and since even your computer and projected colors won't be the same, matching a projected navy blue and printed navy blue will be a time-consuming and frustrating task.

- *For black-and-white printouts:* Because color printing can be expensive, many decks and handouts—especially those designed as backup visuals—are reproduced in black and white. If you are printing with a laser printer, you should be able to use white, black, and two distinct shades of gray. However, if your pages are being photocopied, then you may need to rely on just one gray. Print and check every page to make sure the shading reproduces the way you intended.

Choose visible combinations.   You can't easily see yellow writing on a white page. Nor can you read dark blue print on a black screen. You need far more color contrast to make your words or numbers stand out. Although there are many more options, the following table lists some possible background and text colors:

CONTRASTING COLOR COMBINATIONS	
For a background that is . . .	**. . . use one of these colors for contrast**
Dark blue	White, light to medium yellow, cream, peach, beige, gold, light blue, light green, lavender, pink, or light aqua
Black	White, light to medium yellow, cream, peach, beige, gold, light to medium blue, and other light to medium colors
White	Black, various bright or dark shades of blue, green, purple, red, or brown; shades mixed with gray, like dark gray-blue
Cream	Black, dark to bright blue, dark to bright green, maroon, red, dark brown, dark purple, and other bright or dark colors

When using more than one text color, be sure both your choices contrast with the background and that the two text colors aren't too similar. For example, avoid a light blue title with aqua text.

Choose colors that work together.   Colors not only need to create contrast between the background and foreground, they also need to look good together.

- *Shun the "Crayola effect."* If all the colors have the same intensity— such as fire-engine red, lime green, lemon yellow, and flamingo pink—they will compete with each other, creating a juvenile look, reminiscent of a starter set of Crayola crayons. Don't use more than one very bold hue in your color scheme.

- *Add some muted colors.* Transform garish colors into less jarring ones. To tone down bright colors, mix them with some gray, perhaps choosing maroon instead of bright red or replacing lime green with a subtle shade like sage.

- *Be careful with red and blue.* These two hues are at opposite ends of the light spectrum. When they are placed next to each other on a screen, they seem to vibrate, making it hard to see red lettering on a blue background or red and blue shapes positioned side by side. Avoid this combination for lettering and add a white or black line around a red column placed on a bright blue screen.
- *Try complimentary colors.* Bold opposites (like purple and yellow or blue and orange) can be attractive pairings if you make some adjustments. For instance, combine a purplish-blue background with pale yellow text or use a navy blue background with peach titles. These combinations offer a high degree of contrast and visual interest.

Consider the audience.   People do not view or interpret color the same way. Your audience members will have certain associations with color. Some of their reactions might be based on cultural associations while others are more specific to individuals.

- *National, religious, and other cultural differences:* When you are presenting in a new culture, ask how various colors are viewed. For instance, many people have strong associations with the colors in their country's flag. Similarly, colors may have ceremonial connotations: for example, death is associated with white in some Eastern cultures and yellow in some Moslem cultures. Some colors also have pleasant associations; for example, in Irish lore, green often gets linked to good luck.
- *Business considerations:* Good luck or not, green is often associated with money in the United States because it's the color of the currency. Red, on the other hand, tends to signify loss. Like nations, many companies have colors. When they are multinational organizations, these combinations resonate around the globe (for instance McDonald's gold and red or BP's green and yellow). If you are new to an organization, be careful not to use a competitor's colors as your color scheme.
- *Color blindness:* Even if your corporate colors are red and green, they won't be the right ones to use if your boss can't see the difference. About 5 to 10 percent of the population is color blind; it affects men more often than women. (The inability to distinguish between red and green is the most common type of color blindness.) So, you may want to avoid using red and green column charts. For color-blind people, all those columns might look gray and for others they may signify a holiday season more than profit and loss.

4. Highlight with spot color and animation.

Once you have chosen your background and text colors, think about how you will draw your audiences' attention to a specific place on an individual slide by using: (1) a bright, contrasting "spot color," (2) visual "pointers," (3) segue techniques, and (4) animation to "build" ideas.

Linking spot color to message titles: You can often use spot color to emphasize your main point. For example, to reinforce a message title about "the final stage" or "the East's share of profits," use spot color as illustrated below:

Examples: highlighting to link to message titles

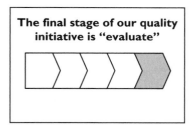
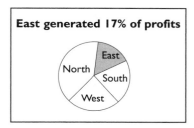

Using spot color and visual elements as a pointer: In the days before PowerPoint, presenters pointed at their overheads or the screen, often with a shaky hand or an even shakier pointer. With PowerPoint, however, you have many more effective ways to "point." For example, you can insert arrows, lines, circles, boxes, symbols, or words to direct your audiences' eyes exactly where you want them to look.

Examples: highlighting as a "pointer"

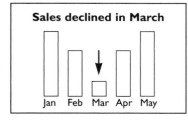

Avoiding the random use of spot color: Don't waste the power of your spot color by using it for unimportant items—such as the bullet character itself, a border, or "fruit salad" PowerPoint defaults that make each pie slice, column, etc. a different color.

Using techniques to segue between sections: You can also use spot color, dimmed color, arrows, or boxes to emphasize your transition from one major section to the next on your repeated preview slide. The examples below illustrate two ways to draw attention to a line of text:

Examples: highlighting for transitions

Our findings revealed major deficiencies 1. Lack of training for section leader 2. Insufficient generators 3. Communication mistakes	**Our findings revealed major deficiencies** 1. Lack of training for section leader 2. Insufficient generators 3. Communication mistakes

Using animation to "build" your ideas: Animation is the PowerPoint tool that allows you to "build"—that is, systematically disclose—one bullet point or image at a time when you are projecting visuals. Use animation in conjunction with your spot color to keep your audience focused on the point you are currently making. If you don't use animation, and simply display the entire slide at once, the audience may read ahead, or become confused or distracted figuring out which point you are discussing. Therefore, think about the best ways to use this function.

- *Build important bullet text.* Your listeners will always read ahead of what you are discussing. Therefore, use builds on any slide you want to emphasize or discuss slowly—such as your preview slide or long, complex lists.

- *Build complex charts.* If you display a complex chart all at once, your listeners may be trying to figure out how your chart works instead of listening to you. Therefore, build the slide gradually, explaining each new element as you add it.

- *Avoid distracting animation.* PowerPoint offers a variety of animation effects—such as dancing text, swirling retreats, flying bullet points, and jarring entrances accompanied by sound (drum rolls, shattered glass, and even wild applause). Avoid silly sound effects and all excessive animation; never choose to have text swooping in from every side; don't make anything flash, swell or spin. These movements distract your audience. Therefore, choose "appear," "wipe right," and other animation effects that won't distract.

5. Add variety with other visual elements.

You can avoid "death by bullet list" by incorporating other visual elements to spice up your slides.

Photographs: Photos can be especially powerful when they fill up the screen. Insert them on a black background and crop them to highlight the right part of the image. You can also add a smaller photo to a bullet list or group several pictures together to add some interest to an important visual.

Maps, drawings, and floor plans: Maps are often used to show travel routes, locations, floor plans, and architectural renderings. As long as maps and drawings are simple, they should project fairly well. Save the detailed versions for decks and handouts.

Logos: Many organizations like to brand their presentation materials with a logo. Be sure to follow corporate identity guidelines when including logos.

Cartoons and clip art: Humor isn't always appropriate. Make sure you know your audience's preferences before you purchase a cartoon for your slide show. And be very careful with clip art. Some of the stock photographs and graphics are appropriately professional, but other images are so silly they might decrease your credibility.

Transitions between slides: We recommend that you transition between each slide using "no transition," "cut," or "wipe right." For those rare times when you want to use a transition to create a memorable effect, remember that simple options are the best. Avoid the whirling, dissolving, diagonally sliding, and overly-dramatic effects that will distract your audience.

Video, animation, and other flourishes: You can add video images to your slide shows to create a change of pace, as discussed on page 42, but avoid prepackaged animation effects, which tend to be overly cute.

To learn how to insert a video clip, adjust a photo, add builds or transitional effects, or make custom colors, see *Guide to PowerPoint,* referenced in the bibliography on page 137.

IV. USE READABLE AND SIMPLE LAYOUTS.

One of the most common problems with visuals is that they can't be read—due to text size, overcrowded slides, and distracting clutter. To avoid these pitfalls, strive for readability and simplicity.

1. Use readable lettering.

To ensure readable lettering, select appropriate fonts, make them large enough to be seen, and use wise formatting options.

Choose one or two fonts.   Computers offer an array of font options. Some are serif fonts, which have extenders at the end of the letters. Others are sans serif fonts, which don't have these flourishes.

You might choose a serif font when you want to create a more traditional looking visual aid, when you're creating a densely-packed handout, or when you're trying to ensure contrast between two fonts. In comparison, sans serif fonts will seem more modern or high tech; they are usually the better option for fonts viewed on a screen. You can compare the traditional look of the serif fonts and the more updated appearance of the sans serif examples below:

Examples of serif fonts:

Times New Roman, Bookman, Garamond

Examples of sans serif fonts:

Arial Narrow, Arial, Verdana

Make sure the lettering is large enough to be seen.   With computer-generated lettering, the minimum font size depends on the font itself and your choice of equipment. For example, if you compare a 20-point Garamond and Verdana font, you'll see the Verdana text is much larger than the Garamond. Similarly, you can fit many more Arial Narrow letters in a limited space than you can regular Arial letters. So font size alone won't determine readability. Nevertheless, based on whether you are projecting or printing your visuals—or even writing by hand—remember the following size guidelines:

- *For projection:* (1) Make titles larger than other text but small enough so you can use message titles—depending on the room, screen size, and the font itself, probably 28 to 36 point; (2) Make the other text smaller than the title but large enough to be seen, perhaps 20 to 24 point; (3) Ensure that labels and sources are visible but do not dominate; they will probably need to be at least 16 point. It's best to test font size in the room with the equipment you'll be using.

- *For decks,* base font size on how the deck is being used. If a deck is the main visual, then use fonts that are large enough for audience members to glance down and easily read the deck. On the other hand, if the deck's only purpose is to document your talk, then you can include more detail and smaller fonts since audience members won't be reading as you speak. Still, be careful with small fonts; older eyes may have trouble seeing tiny 8- to 10-point fonts.

- *For handwritten lettering,* try to keep your letters at least two inches high for every 30 feet of viewing distance. If your handwriting is hard to read or the marker has a fine point, use even larger letters.

Format for readability.   Your computer software tempts you with all sorts of ways to highlight and lay out text. Because all these choices greatly influence readability, keep the following tips in mind:

- *Choose simple highlighting options.* In addition to the plain text, select a simple highlighting style and use it with restraint. Wise highlighting options are boldface text, and in some fonts, italics. Be wary of other options; shadow lettering, outlining, and underlining can actually make your words harder to see. And be especially careful to avoid ***letterjunk:*** the combination of several highlighting styles that overwhelm the eye and decrease readability.

- *Consider your use of case.* For titles, use title case (which capitalizes the first letter of each word) or sentence case (which capitalizes only the first letter of the first word). For bullet lists, choose either sentence case or lower case. Never use all capital letters for anything but short phrases or labels. For proof that capital letters don't make text easier to see, read the following:

A LINE OF CAPITAL LETTERS MAY APPEAR LARGER THAN REGULAR TEXT, BUT USING ALL CAPITAL LETTERS ACUTALLY HURTS READABILITY; THEREFORE, USE CAPITAL LETTERS SPARINGLY.

A line of capital letters may appear larger than regular text, but using all capital letters actually hurts readability; therefore, use capital letters SPARINGLY.

- *Choose left justification.* Message titles look better and are easier to read when they are left justified rather than centered. Also, line up your bullet lists so they are flush with the title. Only use centered text for labels.

- *Select simple bullets.* Choose bullets that are simple and filled (such as ● or ■) and avoid those that call too much attention to themselves (such as ➤ and ❖). If you include subpoints under a major bullet point, then use an even subtler bullet like a dash.

- *Wrap text lines carefully.* Skip two spaces after the bullet point and keep the beginning of all the text lines even. In PowerPoint, you can break and position lines of text by holding down the "Shift" and "Enter" keys together where you want to break a line.

- *Avoid "orphans."* Try not to leave a single word or "orphan" all by itself on a line. Instead, divide the line in a way that makes sense, based on the content.

- *Keep long titles balanced* by dividing them about midway through the message. Left-justified titles tend to look better if the second line is longer than the first one.

2. Watch for wordiness.

Keeping your text charts simple is essential, especially for projected visuals. Just because you *can* fit 14 lines of text on a slide, doesn't mean you *should,* as you can see below.

Ineffective chart: too wordy

Text Visuals Can Hold a Great Deal of Information

- You can put lots of print on a horizontal chart, without wrapping text lines too many times.
- Even if you had 14 lines, you *could* fit them all on a single slide.
- You might even decide to change the line spacing to squeeze in your last idea.
- Your font size might still be readable in the back row. But, nevertheless, the slide still has way too many words on it.
- Writing complete sentences means you can read this wonderful prose to your audience.
- If you make margins really wide and use the space under the bullets, you can squeeze more in, too.

Simplify text visuals. Text visuals are not reports. Nor are they your notes. To simplify them, keep text lines short and limit your bullet points. (You may want to adopt our "six-by-six" guideline for projected slides.) If appropriate, add some active voice, and cut extra text by using "telegram language."

- *Keep text lines short.* With slides, average about six words per line. With decks used as your main visual, average ten words or less per line, and don't run text lines across the entire page. Such long lines are hard to read; instead, use a column layout or leave a very large, right margin. With either slides or decks, if you have long sentences that need to be wrapped to a third line, either simplify the sentence into partial phrases (instead of using complete sentences) or break the line into a main point with subpoints.

- *Limit bullet points.* Using a few subpoints is fine, but don't create subpoints for your subpoints. Once your visual aid becomes nothing more than an outline, it loses visual appeal. If you are using projected visuals, try to limit the number of lines below your title to six.

- *Use the "six-by-six" guideline.* If you combine the suggestions from our two previous points, you'll have a good guideline for designing projected text charts: think 6 × 6—six words per line and six lines per slide. You can violate this guideline every now and then, but if you project three slides in a row, each with more than 36 words, then your audience will be heading for the low point on their attention curve. For decks used as your primary visual, try to limit the number of text lines to ten: think 10 × 10 for a maximum of 100 words per page.

- *Add active voice:* Active voice sends a clear message, while passive voice meanders along, implying your message. Active voice relies on action verbs such as: "decide, "use," and "control," while passive voice softens the statement by relying on weaker verbs such as: "is," "there are," and "might be." Often, passive voice hides the object and uses extra words. For example, assume the title on a deck page reads: "Additional learning will result from the continued use of behavior scan testing." In active voice, this title becomes: "We expect to learn more from behavior scan testing," or "Behavior scan testing assists our research." The switch to active voice speeds the read. For more information about how and when to use active voice, download the plain language guide provided by the Security and Exchange Commission: www/sec.gov/pdf/handbook.pdf.

- *Use "telegram language."* Look ~~out~~ for ~~all these~~ extra words ~~that aren't needed~~. To pare the wording on your visuals, use what expert Charlotte Rosen calls "telegram language"—words that create a clear message, without the extra letters that would make a telegram expensive to send:

Ineffective wordy phrase	*Effective telegram language*
in order to	to
each and every member	members
continue to advocate for	push for
the globalized purchasing efforts	global purchasing

Maintain "stand-alone sense."   Although you want to simplify your text visuals, you don't want to edit them so much that they no longer make stand-alone sense. As explained on page 85, stand-alone sense means your visuals make sense if you aren't there to explain them. When creating deck pages, you can easily include enough detail to make your materials useful for people who didn't attend your talk. However, if you are making slides, you need to carefully balance the need for simplicity with the desire for stand-alone sense. The following examples show how to use wording that clarifies your message:

Ineffective bullet text: *Lacks stand-alone sense*	*Effective bullet text:* *Makes stand-alone sense*
• Marketing report	• Large market with unmet needs
• Competitive analysis	• No direct competition in St. Louis
• Operational changes	• Logistics software to reduce inventory

3. Delete chartjunk.

To use the term coined by design guru Edward Tufte, delete "chartjunk"—that is, any extraneous design elements that do not contribute to your message. Regain control of your slides and deck pages by modifying the chartjunk defaults inherent in PowerPoint:

- *Change default settings.* (1) Avoid the "fruit salad effect" and control the use of spot color. (2) Eliminate any items that do not add meaning— including grid lines, tick marks, cross-hatching, borders, unnecessary shading, and redundant titles.

- *Get rid of legends.* Legends slow down your viewers; therefore, insert labels manually on or near pie slices or next to the lines on a line chart.

- *Use 2D, not 3D.* To avoid misleading your audience, always choose two-dimensional, rather than three-dimensional, views.

- *Modify width, spacing, and boldness.* Modify chart elements to (1) make skinny bars and columns wider and decrease the space between them (the space between them should be less than their width) and (2) increase the boldness of trend lines to make them visible.

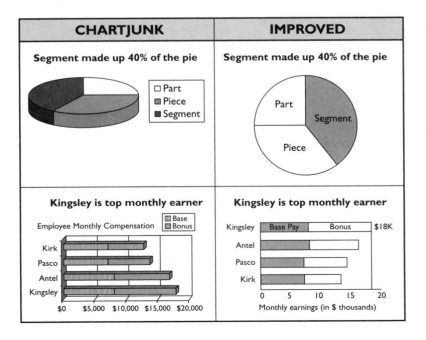

V. BE CONSISTENT AND CORRECT.

Make sure all your slides or deck pages are consistent and correct: (1) use a template so your visuals have a unified look, (2) ensure structural consistency by using your preview visual effectively, and (3) check every visual, paying special attention to your lists.

1. Design your own template.

Your visual aids need to look coherent as a group. If you are using PowerPoint, you can create a template to guarantee that the same color scheme and design elements appear on all your slides or deck pages. By designing this "master slide," not only will you ensure visual consistency, but you will also simplify the task of preparing your visuals.

Strive for a consistent visual image.   (1) *Team consistency:* If you are preparing a team presentation, make sure everyone works with the same template; otherwise, the visuals will end up looking as if they were thrown together. (2) *Organizational consistency:* Perhaps your organization has provided you with a design template or some color guidelines. If so, follow them carefully. Organizations, like individuals, benefit from using consistent visual communication.

Create a template.   To design a template, choose your color scheme, the size and placement of your title, the fonts you want to use, the size and color of the text in your bullet lists, the type of bullets, and so on.

Why should you design your own template when the software has dozens available? The reason is that most PowerPoint templates are full of distractions. Many include distracting graphics that interfere with your text and charts. Others use all-over background patterns, such as shimmers, textures, or fades that can make the text hard to read. All of them use title fonts that are much too large for message titles, and many have distracting font styles and bullets. Although you can simplify some PowerPoint templates to make them usable, usually it takes the same amount of time to design your own.

Be cautious if using prepared templates. While we recommend creating your own template, if you are new to PowerPoint, you may feel you need to use one of the templates that come with the program. (1) *Avoid the exceptionally distracting templates:* While it's obvious you won't want to use a template that seems designed for a kindergarten class, you also want to steer clear of those with all-over background designs. The ribbons, swirls, grids, and other patterns are especially annoying when they are printed as black-and-white handouts. (2) *Change the color scheme:* With every template, you can choose a variety of prepared color schemes. Some need a little tweaking, perhaps making the spot color match your logo. Others should be skipped entirely, either because they fail to provide contrast between the text and background or because they use wild color combinations that go well beyond the fruit salad effect.

2. Ensure structural consistency.

Your preview visual is the key component in ensuring structural consistency. Whether you think of it as an agenda slide or the table of contents in a deck, design and use your preview visual so that it makes your structure clear. Here are three possible ways to increase its effectiveness: (1) repeat the preview between each main section of your presentation, (2) add trackers that correspond to your preview, (3) make your preview visual stand out by adding some visual interest and using a message title instead of a topic title such as, "agenda" or "preview."

Repeat your preview between each section. In a long slide presentation, one way to emphasize structure and consistency is to return to the preview slide—highlighting the new section as you move through your talk. If your preview is a bullet list, you can highlight it as shown on page 96: by placing a box around the upcoming section or by "dimming" the text of the sections that are not going to be featured.

Add trackers.   Another way to reinforce the structure of a long presentation is to use trackers—words or symbols that identify the section of the talk. Trackers often appear in the corners or bottom of a slide or deck page. They need to be visible, but avoid making them so large that they compete with other text.

You can't add trackers to a template; instead, you need to insert them individually, on every slide or page, toward the end of the design process. Here are two slides that include trackers:

Tracker examples: word lower right and symbols at bottom

Northern region showed dramatic improvements
• New hires contributed as trainees • Expenses held steady • Profit margins were exceptional
Northern

Eastern region faces multiple challenges
• Turnover rate exceeded 15% • Travel expenses double • Profits were disappointing
N–S–**E**–W

Make your preview slide stand out.   A bullet list can work just fine as a preview, especially if you include some sort of graphic or design element to differentiate it from your other lists. Alternatively, you might want to use a concept chart as your preview visual.

The table on the facing page shows examples of lists transformed into images that attract more attention. Note that all these preview visuals use message titles rather than a single word such as "agenda."

EXAMPLES OF PREVIEW VISUALS: TEXT VS. IMAGE	
Preview text visuals . . .	**. . . transformed**
Wind power is a good option for Point Hope 1. High-paying, local jobs 2. Carbon-free, clean energy 3. Subsidized investment	**Wind power** → ① High-paying, local jobs / ② Carbon-free, clean energy / ③ Subsidized investment **. . . a good option for Point Hope**
Improve growth and efficiency at Bard Company • Target new customers • Consolidate operations • Change product mix	Target new customers → **Improve Bard's Growth and Efficiency** ← Change product mix / Consolidate operations

3. Check every visual.

The last refinements involve checking for consistency and correctness: maintain consistent phrasing, document your sources, confirm that each slide or page is free of typos or formatting errors, and check your lists to make sure they use parallel structure.

Maintain consistent phrasing. Use the same wording throughout your talk that you did in your preview. For instance, if you list "financial projections" on your preview, don't switch to "spreadsheet analysis" in the title of your supporting visual. Similarly, if using trackers, mirror the wording used on your preview visual. For example, although it would be fine to write "Northern region" on your preview slide and use the word "Northern" as a tracker, you wouldn't want to write "Mid-Atlantic region" on your preview slide and use the word "East" as your tracker because the connection between the tracker and the words on the slide is not exceptionally clear.

Document your sources. If you are using a chart, cite any numbers that come from outside the organization. Don't use data from unknown or suspect sources. Similarly, if you use an expert's words, identify them as that person's ideas and not your own. On projected visuals, use limited citations, perhaps just noting the author's last name. On decks, you can include more detailed information; consider including a bibliography in the appendix.

Check for errors. Double-check all the data you used to create your charts; ask someone else to proofread your slides and deck pages. A typo on a page is annoying; one that is projected six-inches high on a screen is far worse. It can be a credibility-killer for someone in the audience to spot an inaccurate number and more than a little embarrassing to spot a misspelled word as you are walking the decision maker through a page of your deck. Also check for formatting errors: align text and images properly and search for extra spaces in text charts.

Check your lists. After you have pared down your bullet lists, as described on pages 101–102, have someone read them and ask whether they make stand-alone sense. Also check your lists for (1) grammatical parallelism and (2) "conceptual parallelism," a term coined by communication expert Jo Anne Yates.

- *Use grammatical parallelism.* Make sure the first word in a series uses the same part of speech as the other first words in the series. In other words, if your first three bullet points begin with an action verb, your last point shouldn't start with the phrase "how to . . ." Similarly, if your first subpoint is a noun, the next one needs to be a noun, too.

Example: ineffective grammatical parallelism

- New health-care plans are available
- To qualify for prescription drug benefits
- About your pension fund

Example: effective grammatical parallelism

- Reviewing the new health-care plans
- Qualifying for prescription drug benefits
- Learning more about your pension fund

- *Ensure conceptual parallelism.* Sometimes a main idea gets mixed in with subpoints or the real title for your slide isn't on the top after all; instead, you discover it at the beginning or end of a list. To ensure conceptual consistency, go back and check your lists. Make sure you haven't mixed main and lesser points.

Example of ineffective conceptual parallelism

Design Your Visuals

- Follow five design guidelines
- Decide on the type of visual aid
- Begin with your message titles
- Think visually as you design
- Use readable and simple layouts
- Ensure consistency and correctness

Example of effective conceptual parallelism

Follow Five Design Guidelines for Visuals

- Decide on the type of visual aid
- Begin with your message titles
- Think visually as you design
- Use readable and simple layouts
- Ensure consistency and correctness

Not only is the final list conceptually parallel, but it is also a fitting way to close this chapter. Remember this list of guidelines when you design your visuals. If you follow these five guidelines, you will create visuals that enhance your presentation and help you accomplish your objective.

CHAPTER 6 OUTLINE

I. ANALYZE YOUR NONVERBAL STYLE.
  1. Body position and movement
  2. Hand and arm gestures
  3. Eye contact and facial expression
  4. Vocal traits
  5. Space and objects around you

II. PRACTICE YOUR NONVERBAL DELIVERY.
  1. Check your content and timing.
  2. Rehearse with your visuals.

III. MANAGE YOUR NERVOUS SYMPTOMS.
  1. General techniques
  2. Physical techniques
  3. Mental techniques
  4. Last-minute tips

CHAPTER 6

Refine Your Nonverbal Delivery

The third part of implementation focuses on your nonverbal skills—how you look and sound to your audience. We all know that nonverbal elements are crucial to a presentation's success. Even so, "perfect" delivery is not necessary. In fact, it's not even possible since different people prefer different delivery styles.

Although you always want to look and sound natural, you will want to adapt your delivery to the formality of the situation. With practice, you should be able to develop a range of effective delivery behaviors that all look and sound like you. As you work on your delivery, use the suggestions in this chapter to (1) analyze your nonverbal style, (2) practice your nonverbal delivery, and (3) manage your nervous symptoms.

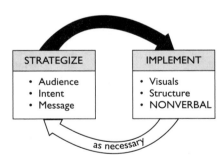

I. ANALYZE YOUR NONVERBAL STYLE.

Many nonverbal elements affect your delivery. Some are your own behaviors, such as your gesturing habits and facial expression. You can observe these by watching yourself on videotape or rehearsing in front of a mirror. Other nonverbal elements are separate from you, such as the objects in the room and the distance between you and your audience. You will become more aware of these nonverbal elements if you rehearse in the place where you will be presenting. All of these nonverbal behaviors are situational: they vary by personality, room size, audience, and culture.

1. Body position and movement

You communicate a great deal just by how you position and move your body.

Distracting positions are often obvious from the start of a presentation. Where you position your legs and feet affects your whole body and influences how you move.

- *The informal "hip sit":* Many presenters like to rest their weight on one leg. If you "park on your hip," your stance will look informal. The distractions tend to begin when your legs get tired: if you start switching back and forth, from one leg to the other, the unintended motion can attract unwanted attention.

- *Problematic foot placement:* If you stand with your feet too far apart, you will look like a ranch hand doing the "cowpoke straddle." However, if you place your feet too close together, you will look timid and submissive. In addition, check your toes: if they are pointed away from your heels, in a "duck stance," you may look as if you are waddling when you walk.

- *Leaning troubles:* Leaning positions like the "podium clutch" and "table lean," leave your legs and feet free to do distracting things—such as swing, wrap, twist, or tap.

- *Moving mistakes:* Watch for distracting motion, such as bouncing, rocking, and pacing. Also avoid taking single steps up and back or side to side. Such, repetitive, purposeless motion distracts the audience.

- *Sloppy sitting:* Check how people sit around a conference table. Slouching doesn't look professional. Swiveling soon gets distracting.

Effective formal positions usually involve standing because being above your audience creates a more formal environment than being seated at the same level. Standing on a stage, behind a podium, creates an exceptionally formal look. But even when you are standing directly in front of a group, you need to know how to use a solid opening stance and combine it with movement that is appropriate for the situation.

- *Position your legs and feet formally.* To create a formal opening stance: (1) place your feet about shoulder-width apart, rather than very close together or far apart; (2) distribute your weight evenly, using both legs equally for support; (3) divide your weight between your heels and the balls of your feet; (4) make sure your feet are straight, avoiding a "duck" position by keeping your feet parallel; and (5) don't lock your knees. This position tends to feel awkward until you get used to it, but it looks good and prevents unintended movement.

- *Return to the formal stance after you move.* In formal situations, it's fine to move for a reason—to emphasize a point on your visual aid, for example, or to move closer to the audience to signal that you are seeking questions. Just make sure your feet are in the formal position described above once you have finished moving.

Effective informal positions include many more options. If you are standing, you can signal that you want to create an informal exchange by leaning momentarily against a table or using a more casual posture. You might also choose to present from a chair.

Environmental factors influence where you stand and how you move: (1) *Room size* is one consideration. For example, in a large room, one effective way to use movement is to walk from one side of the room to the other to indicate that you are beginning a new section of your presentation. (2) *Seating arrangements* may also be a factor. For example, in a "U-shape" arrangement, you don't want to spend too much time in the center of the room since people on the side will only have a view of your back.

Personal style also affects movement. Some people have lots of energy and prefer to move around the room; they need to be careful not to walk too much and to remain still at times, giving the audience a break from all that motion. Other presenters prefer to stay in one place, sometimes seeking safety behind a podium; they may want to walk to a new place, when appropriate, to add variety to their delivery.

2. Hand and arm gestures

Many presenters find that their hands and arms feel very awkward when they present: they don't know where to put their hands, and their arms suddenly feel too long. To use effective gestures, we suggest you (1) discover your natural gesturing style, (2) avoid distracting gestures, (3) use conversational patterns, and (4) adapt to the situation.

Discover your natural gesturing style.   To do so, get a sense of your gesturing habits in various situations, such as when you are talking at a cocktail party or across a dinner table. Ask people who know you to comment on how often you gesture and which gestures you tend to use. Inquire about the size of your gestures, and find out about any distracting arm, hand, or finger habits. Even better, arrange to be videotaped so you can see how you gesture for yourself.

Avoid distracting gestures.   Once you learn about your natural gesturing habits, you will want to eliminate distracting gestures and avoid overusing your favorites. Some small, repetitive, gestures are signs of stress. These nervous fidgets include touching your hair, rubbing your face, and twisting your ring, just to describe a few. In addition, many hand and arm positions have descriptive or humorous names; they tend to send the wrong nonverbal message to the audience.

- *The commander* places her hands on her hips.
- *The chilly presenter* crosses his arms over his chest.
- *The gun-shot victim* clings to her upper arm with one hand.
- *The armless presenter* leaves his hands behind his back.
- *The exposed presenter* clasps her hand in front of her, where a "figleaf" would be.
- *The pocket jingler* puts his hands in his pockets, shaking keys and coins.
- *The clutcher* grasps a pen or pointer and never puts the object down.
- *The slapper* makes noise as she slaps her palms against her thighs.

Use conversational patterns.   Aside from avoiding distracting gestures, you want your gesturing style as a speaker to match the style you use in conversations. If possible, you also want to use some emphatic gestures.

- *Emphasize your message.* Some gestures go along with your verbal content, adding nonverbal reinforcement to your message. For example, if you are "balancing two issues," your palms might be turned up, alternately moving up and down to simulate a scale. Try not to force such gestures. The best emphatic gestures are those you really tend to use.

- *Avoid extremes.* Most of your gestures should be below your face and above your waist. Watch for extremes: if you use lots of huge gestures that extend down to your knees and over your head, you may look more like a cheerleader than a business presenter. On the other hand, if you keep your hands at your sides and use only tiny movements, you may resemble a flapping penguin.

- *Point appropriately.* Reserve pointing for visual aids, not for people. Or try "friendly pointing" that uses your whole hand, keeping your palm sidewise or tilted slightly up and your fingers together.

- *Refine, but don't obsess.* Remember, you don't need to be perfect. You might fidget once, slap your thigh, overuse your favorite gesture, and still accomplish your presentation objective. Practice to refine your gesturing style, but don't obsess about it.

Adapt to the situation. Although you want them to be natural, your gestures should also be influenced by the environment and the audience.

- *Consider room size.* In a large room, gestures can be big and still look appropriate; however, speaking in a small space or on a TV screen requires smaller gestures.

- *Think about your audience.* Some people like presenters who gesture often. Others prefer limited gesturing. You can't please everyone, so usually it's best to use your own style. However, if you see that people are staring at your hands, perhaps you'll want to scale back some of your gesturing. Similarly, if you tend to look a bit too formal, adding a few gestures, especially friendly "palms up" gestures, can make your style seem less rigid.

- *Consider cultural norms.* In some cultures, expansive gestures are common, while in other cultures gesturing tends to be far more restrained. One of the most important cultural differences to consider involves hand signals that stand on their own. What you use to show "OK" may not mean "everything is all right" in some cultures. Similarly, the "thumbs up" and "stop" signals have various meanings. Be very careful when using such gestures in cross-cultural situations; you don't want to unintentionally send an insulting or even vulgar message.

3. Eye contact and facial expression

Your face plays a crucial role in your nonverbal delivery style: your eye contact connects you to your audience, and your face communicates interest, confidence, and enthusiasm.

Eye contact: Most U.S. business audiences want you to "look them in the eye"—a mark of honesty and confidence according to cultural norms. Here are some tips to assist you as you use eye contact to connect with your audience:

- *Find a friendly face.* If you are nervous, making eye contact with a supportive person might actually calm you down. The smiles and nods you see from the friendly face can help you get through the difficult parts of your presentation and boost your confidence.

- *Have "little conversations."* Imagine you are speaking to one person at a time so you will feel less intimidated by a large audience and be able to develop a more natural delivery style.

- *Look long enough to complete a thought.* You don't want to stare. But you don't want your eye contact to be darting. Therefore, look at a person's whole face—not just the pupils—and look long enough to complete a thought or register a reaction.

- *Locate influential audience members.* When delivering a persuasive presentation, check the reactions of the decision makers and other people with influence. However, don't focus on these people to the extent that others may feel excluded.

- *Use your body as you make eye contact.* In a wide room, if you only move your head from one side to the other, the audience will begin to feel as if they are watching you watch a tennis match. To overcome this problem, turn more than just your neck and head when you look from side to side and connect with people sitting in the middle as you move your eye contact across the room.

- *Make adjustments for large audiences.* If you are speaking before a crowd of hundreds, try to find one person in each section of the audience to use as an anchor point for your eye contact. If you then start looking at people sitting around these anchors, you can be sure you aren't ignoring part of the audience. When lighting prevents you from seeing anyone, you still need to give the appearance of making eye contact throughout the room.

Facial expression: What the audience sees on your face will affect how they hear your message. Try to avoid the stony, deadpan expression of ineffective speakers. Instead, relax your face and use natural expressions that are appropriate for your message.

- *Use conversational facial expression.* Like gesturing, facial expression is very speaker specific. Use your natural expressions to connect with the audience.

- *Smile when appropriate.* Conversational facial expression does not mean you have to smile all the time. For example, you might want to smile when you introduce yourself, but avoid smiling out of nervousness or when discussing sad or serious topics.

- *Interact with the audience.* Try the technique of looking at someone in the audience with "appropriate" facial expression and mirror the look on that person's face. For example, if you want to remember to smile, look at a friendly face; that person's smile might help you express one of your own.

4. Vocal traits

Your voice should sound natural and interesting. To achieve this sound, avoid reading or memorizing. Reading causes most people to stumble over words and use unnatural vocal patterns. Memorizing leads to an artificial style because it usually sounds rehearsed. Instead, use a natural-sounding style. To do so, become aware of the elements that make up your vocal image, such as volume, rate, inflection, and enunciation. You'll want to vary the first three and enunciate in a way that suits the formality of the situation.

Volume: Your volume is determined by how loudly or softly you speak. You need to be loud enough for everyone to hear you, but you don't want to overwhelm people with sound. Many people can't accurately assess their volume so it's a good idea to go to the presentation room ahead of time with a friend; ask this person to stand in the back so you can test your volume. If you have a booming voice, you may want to lower the sound level a bit. If your volume is low, know that your voice will be even harder to hear once people fill the room. Since too little volume, rather than too much, tends to be an issue for many speakers, here are some tips to make sure you can be heard:

- *Speak to the back row.* If you have a soft, hard-to-hear voice, begin by speaking to the person farthest away from you and try not to let this volume drop.

- *Avoid vocal strain.* Learn how to increase volume without creating vocal strain. Begin by pretending that you are perched on a balcony, with the audience sitting below. When you attempt to send your voice downward, you will produce sound by pushing from your diaphragm rather than your throat. Your volume will increase, but you won't sound as if you are shouting. Even better, you won't strain your vocal cords.

- *Listen for "volume drops."* Volume sometimes drops to inaudible levels in two situations: (1) *At the end of sentences:* If your voice trails off at the end of sentences, try pausing as you complete a sentence; take in enough air to keep your volume strong all the way to the end of the sentence. (2) *As you introduce a new visual aid:* If people can't hear you when you introduce a new visual aid, either try talking to the people in the back row or pause if you need to turn away to put up a new visual.

- *Vary volume.* Try to vary your volume to add interest. If you say some words or phrases with extra volume, you can emphasize them. For speakers with loud voices, sometimes lowering the sound level can also get attention.

- *Test the microphone.* If a microphone is creating volume for you, practice with it. You won't want to get too close or you'll hear a horrible screeching sound.

Rate: Your rate involves the speed of your delivery—how quickly or slowly you say your words and how and when you insert pauses.

- *Slow down if you talk too fast.* When some speakers feel anxious or excited, they tend to speak faster than usual. If you are one of these fast talkers, you will want to slow your pace when you are presenting. Try rehearsing your presentation at an artificially slow rate; as you present, you will recall this rehearsal rate and have an easier time slowing down.

- *Add pauses to slow your rate.* One of the best ways to slow your overall rate is to use more pauses. To do so, try to get comfortable with silence. Add an audible pause at the end of a sentence. Use this time to breathe deeply before you begin speaking again. Also pause briefly for commas, and try inserting a pause before and after an important message. Pausing will make your points stand out.

- *Speed up if you talk too slowly.* If you speak at a very slow rate, try to speed up at times, for instance, when the material is simple. You might also try to vary other elements of your voice, such as inflection, to make your voice sound lively.

- *Adjust for cultural differences.* (1) Alter your rate so that it is appropriate for the culture. For example, in the Northeastern region of the United States, a fairly rapid rate is the norm; however, in the South, most people speak more slowly. (2) Consider your accent: if your accent isn't familiar to your audience, then slow down, especially at the beginning, so people can get used to your speech patterns. (3) Remember non-native speakers: slow down and make other adjustments as noted on page 12 to help listeners who are learning the language.

Inflection: We use the word "inflection" to refer to speaking with variation in your pitch.

- *Speak with expressiveness and enthusiasm,* in a warm, pleasant tone, with pitch variety to create a lively and energetic delivery.

- *Avoid speaking in a monotone.* The opposite of effective inflection is a dull, robotic monotone that makes you sound as if you are bored. To improve a monotone voice, try saying long lists of words or numbers, using your voice to say some items with a high note and others with a low note. Once you've mastered making a list sound intriguing, you can then decide which messages in your presentation need the same sort of vocal emphasis.

- *Add low notes to a high-pitched voice.* Deep voices tend to be heard as more authoritative than higher-pitched ones. So, if you have a very high voice, you will want to learn how to lower your pitch and eliminate any shrill-sounding tones. To do so, practice diaphragmatic breathing as explained on page 131.

- *Avoid turning statements into questions.* When you make a statement, your voice goes down at the end of the sentence. When you ask a question, you use upward inflection. Some people unintentionally turn statements into questions, ending far too many sentences on a high note, which can make them sound unsure of themselves and decrease their credibility. To avoid this problem, practice driving inflection downward at the end of sentences.

Enunciation: Also known as "articulation," enunciation refers to how clearly you say your words. Whether you enunciate formally or informally should depend on the nature of your presentation.

- *To use formal enunciation,* you need to speak carefully, saying all your consonants and making sure your vowels are heard. Avoid dropping final letters, (so that "talking" becomes "talkin") or squeezing words together (so that "going to" sounds like "gunna").

- *In less formal situations,* using such careful enunciation can make you sound stiff. While you do want to make sure your words can be understood, you don't need to use such precise articulation. In these cases, you can use contractions, replacing "do not" with "don't" and "you will" with "you'll" to create a breezier style.

- *To avoid stumbling over words,* in either formal or informal situations, identify the words that cause you trouble. For example, perhaps the word "similarly" is hard for you to say. If so, breathe before you use this word and think about each syllable as you say it. Sometimes you can rely on a synonym, perhaps using "likewise" to make your job easier.

Filler words and sounds: These verbal pauses are words and sounds that creep into your speech. Along with stutters, stumbles, and poor enunciation, they hurt the smoothness of your delivery. Some common fillers are *uh, er, um,* and *you know.* Using a few *ums* is natural for many speakers; if used only occasionally, they are not a problem. However, if used repeatedly, these words and sounds can become a distraction.

- *Add pauses to cut back on filler words and sounds.* If you overuse fillers, try to add pauses to replace some of them. Also attempt to become comfortable with silence; some people insert fillers because the lack of sound bothers them.

- *Listen for advanced filler words.* Some speakers have developed what communication expert Joann Baney calls "advanced filler words." These speakers create amazingly long compound, complex sentences by avoiding pauses and inserting words such as *and* or *so.* They may also use needless phrases such as "to be honest . . ." (which may make them sound less than honest) or "as a matter of fact . . ." (which can be omitted and replaced with the fact).

5. Space and objects around you

Other nonverbal elements have to do with the space and objects around you.

Space: Check out the size and shape of the room, its furnishings, and the distance between you and the audience. All these elements will affect your presentation.

- *Consider the seating arrangement.* Straight lines of chairs create a formal environment. On the other hand, a horseshoe or U-shape arrangement encourages participation and creates a less formal atmosphere. Even the shape of a table matters; for instance, presenting at a round table seems less formal than choosing to sit at the head of a long, rectangular one.

- *Factor in height and distance.* The higher you are in relationship to your audience, the more formal the atmosphere you establish nonverbally. Therefore, the most formal presentations might be delivered from a stage or platform. In a semiformal situation, you might stand while the audience sits. To make a situation even less formal, you might sit with your audience at a table or in a circle of chairs. Distance is also linked to formality. The farther you are away from the audience, the more formal you will appear.

Objects: Think also about the objects you choose to have around you, including what you wear.

- *Objects between you and the audience:* To increase formality, use objects (such as a podium or table) to separate yourself from your audience. To decrease formality, don't place objects between yourself and the audience.

- *Visual aids:* Interacting with your visual aids affects your delivery as detailed on pages 124–127. If used poorly, your visuals can become an unintended barrier between you and the audience.

- *Dress:* Think about the audience's expectations and choose apparel that is right for the occasion, the organization, and the culture. For instance, what is appropriate to fashion editors may be totally unacceptable to investment bankers. Similarly, a suit that works great for an interview may look out of place on casual Friday. Avoid apparel that draws too much attention—such as exaggerated, dangling jewelry or loud, flashy ties. Dress to project the image you want to create, one that will enhance your credibility.

II. PRACTICE YOUR NONVERBAL DELIVERY.

You can enhance your delivery by using the rehearsal techniques covered in this section.

1. Check your content and timing.

Instead of reading verbatium from your slides or from word-for-word notes, prepare limited notes and rehearse out loud to become aware of content, timing, and nonverbal issues.

Using an outline for your speaking notes: Some presenters like to present from an outline. However, an outline used for speaking notes needs to be streamlined by:

- *Writing phrases only:* Don't use complete sentences; instead print very short phrases for your main points and subpoints.

- *Using large lettering:* Make sure you can see your outline from arm's length. Leave lots of white space so it is easy to read.

- *Inserting delivery reminders:* You can add reminders, such as "speak slowly" or "show line chart now." These notes can help you remember what you are supposed to do as well as say.

- *Using note cards:* Most experts favor note cards over paper, suggesting that you put your revised presentation outline on 5 × 7 or 4 × 6 inch cards. You can handwrite these notes or print them from a computer, using a large font. Note cards have many advantages: they are easier to hold than paper if you want to move around as you present; they allow you to rearrange your materials easily; and their small size limits how much you can put on them. Typically, one note card should hold about five minute's worth of presentation reminders.

Making notes based on your visual aids: Other presenters prefer to print out copies of their visual aids and use these images as the basis of their notes. Sometimes they print their slides two-per-page and then add their speaking notes. If you use this technique, cut the paper into half sheets to avoid holding the floppy and unprofessional-looking large sheets. As another option, you might print your slides four per page, attaching each of the smaller images to a note card and including reminders below the images.

Rehearsing: Once you have your notes, you are ready to rehearse. If the material is complicated and new, you will likely need to run through it more than once, timing yourself to ensure that you won't run overtime. If your presentation is similar to one you have given many times before, you may only need to practice a few of the important elements, such as your opening, your closing, and the transitions you plan to use between sections.

- *Rehearse out loud.* In all cases, practice out loud. Knowing your content is not the same as saying it. So, don't just read over your notes: say the material out loud, using the vocal traits you want to use on the day of your talk.

- *Rehearse on your feet.* If you will be standing when you speak, then get on your feet when you rehearse.

- *Make adjustments:* An initial rehearsal will point out where your structure is weak, if you are missing transitions, and if you have too much material. In following rehearsals, you can focus on polishing your nonverbal skills and becoming comfortable with your visual aids (as described on pages 124–127).

Timing a rehearsal: Time control is important. Running overtime can annoy your audience and undercut your credibility. Only by practicing your entire presentation out loud, can you effectively check your timing. If you plan to use visual aids, rehearse with them to make sure you have time to introduce and show them all.

- *Time each section.* If you are rehearsing on your own, practice each section by itself and note how long it takes. Or better yet, videotape your rehearsal so you will be able to document the length of each section. As another option, ask someone to attend your rehearsal and time the various sections of your talk. With this information, you can make better choices about how to cut material.

- *Plan to finish early.* If your rehearsal reveals that you will end almost exactly on time, you still need to make cuts. Factor in the time you will need to respond to questions and the time your audience will need to understand your visual aids.

- *Decide how to make additional cuts.* Prepare to adjust timing further, if necessary, during your presentation. If you run short on time, do not rush through your points. Instead, plan to cut details and emphasize key messages.

2. Rehearse with your visuals.

Using visuals affects the timing of your presentation, but you also need to practice with them so you can gracefully integrate them into the flow of your talk.

Practicing with the equipment: Become extremely comfortable with the equipment you have decided to use. Practicing is especially important with high-tech visuals and equipment you haven't used before. Don't lose credibility by fumbling with cords and searching in vain for the power switch. Instead, check out the equipment: set it up, turn it on, press the buttons, use the remote, insert and play the video, flip the pages, position the slides, and so on.

Introducing each visual.   Even well-designed visuals don't speak for themselves; it's your job to help them communicate your message.

- *State your transition, then the main message.* To do so, segue from your current topic to the message you plan to show with your visual aid. For example, you might ask: "So what were sales results for the last quarter?" Then, pause to put up your visual, allowing your audience to see it, before saying: "Here you see that the Southwest office reached their $6 million goal."

- *Give the audience time.* Remember your audience has never seen your visual aid before; therefore, it will take them longer to grasp the meaning of your slide or deck page than it will take you.

- *Explain complex visuals.* When showing complex charts or diagrams, introduce the main idea and then explain the meaning of any symbols, colors, axes, or labels you have used. When possible, build complex images so you can provide this background information as you add various elements to the chart or diagram.

- *Cue the audience.* Don't assume people will know where they are supposed to look. Tell them. Show them. Or do both.

Controlling visual distractions.   Get rid of old visuals and glaring, white screens. Also be careful not to let your visuals distract you.

- *Eliminate "old news."* Once you are done with an image, remove it. You don't want to talk about a new idea while everyone is looking at an old visual. You also don't want a blank white screen behind you, so turn off the overhead projector, insert a plain, black slide into your slide show, or use the blank screen command on your remote (or the "B" key on your keyboard) to make the screen unobtrusive.

- *Talk to and look at the audience.* Visuals can become eye-contact magnets; don't let them disconnect you from your audience. For example, if you are writing on a board, don't write and talk at the same time. Otherwise, the audience will only see your back and might miss what you are trying to say. Similarly, don't look over your shoulder and talk to a screen. Practice until you will be able to focus your attention on your audience and not your visual aids.

Showing computer-generated slides: Computer-generated slide shows are among the most commonly used visual aids in corporate presentations. In addition to preparing a back-up handout to use in case of an emergency, remember these slide show tips:

- *Check the equipment.* Save your slide show on the computer's hard drive so it will run faster than if you use a memory drive or CD and practice with the cordless mouse. If using a laptop, turn off screen savers and the power-saving mode that will change your screen after a certain amount of time.

- *Check your slides.* Test the colors and transitions to make sure your slides appear the way you intended. In most cases, the colors you see on your computer will not match those projected on the screen. Next, walk to the back of the room. Verify that all the lettering is easy to see and every slide is free of mistakes.

- *Practice introducing and building each visual.* Follow the tips on page 124 to integrate your slides into your talk. Go over all the cueing features you have inserted (such as the "build and dim" feature often used to add bullet points). Check the animation you have used to build complex charts or diagrams.

- *Insert extra slides at the end.* Either make extra copies of your final slide or insert several black slides at the end of your slide show to make sure an extra click on the remote won't send you out of slide show mode and back to the PowerPoint program. Endings are important, so guarantee that your closing message—and not the PowerPoint program—will have the spotlight.

Presenting with a deck: No matter how they are going to be used, decks need to be carefully proofread before they are printed. Check each copy to make sure the pages are in order and nothing has been left out. The following tips apply for times when a deck is your primary visual:

- *Preview with the table of contents.* Include a table of contents in your deck, and review it with the audience. For example, you might say: "As you can see in the table of contents, this deck has four sections. In the next hour, I'll (1) explain why the timing and environment are right for this new venture, (2) share some financial information that should interest you, (3) take you through our competitive analysis, and (4) introduce you to the other members of the management team who can turn this business plan into a profitable reality."

- *Explain how you plan to use the deck.* Let the audience know if you plan to go over all the pages or only a few. If you have included an appendix, tell them what's in it and how the material should be used.

- *Be flexible.* Deck presentations are supposed to be flexible and interactive. Be responsive to your audience by skipping a page that turns out to be unnecessary or jumping to a new section if appropriate.

- *Let listeners know where you are.* Help the audience follow along, by saying something such as: "As you'll see on page 17, most of our competition would be larger and far less flexible organizations . . ."

- *Introduce each new page.* Begin by highlighting the main message, which should be conveniently located in your title. If necessary, explain your use of color and the elements of your charts or diagrams. For example, you might say, "Down the left side of the matrix, I have listed the five skills or traits we are looking for in an applicant . . ." or "The green bars on this chart show the base pay for each member of the sales team . . ."

- *Don't read from the deck.* Talk to your audience and not the paper. If possible, place the deck on a table so you can gesture. Direct their attention to the deck pages only when necessary. At other times make eye contact with the audience to keep their focus on you and not the visual aid. If a deck page has lots of print on it, do not read the text to your audience. Instead, give them time to read it for themselves or summarize it for them.

Using flip charts: Use flip charts to make your presentation interactive by recording people's comments, or use them as prepared visuals for small, informal groups.

- *Write so they can read it.* Choose thick markers in visible colors and have spare ones nearby. Include message titles if they will fit on the page. (If your writing is messy or you want to save time, prepare your titles ahead or have someone write them for you.)

- *Practice flipping pages.* Turning a page on a large flip chart can be difficult. Practice until you can do it with one motion. To make it easier to find a prepared page, bend the corner of the page on top of it. Label the upturned corner in pencil. When you're ready to show the prepared page, it will be easy to find because of the upturned corner.

- *Decide what to do with old news.* Once a page is no longer needed, flip it so the audience isn't distracted by an old list. On the other hand, if you want the audience to recall several pages, remove them from the pad and use tape to hang them somewhere in the room.

- *Remain focused on the audience.* Avoid writing and talking simultaneously. Instead, stop talking. Write on the flip chart. And stand to the side so the audience can see what you've written. When recording someone else's thoughts, try to look at the person as long as possible before breaking the connection to write on the flip chart. Check back when you're done to make sure you got it right.

Using overhead projectors: Although they are rarely used in formal presentations, some presenters still like this older technology. They can be prepared ahead and printed from a computer or used to record comments during your talk. To use overheads effectively:

- *Avoid blocking people's view.* Check to see if the arm of the projector blocks anyone's view. Also, position yourself so you won't be in the way: move back toward the screen.

- *Cue the audience.* Stand to the left of the screen and use your left hand to point to the beginning of a text line or the specific place you want the audience to look.

- *Be prepared.* Ask where the spare bulb is kept and test that it works. If the projector is rickety, figure out how to prop it up so the image isn't "keyed" (wider at the top than the bottom) or crooked.

III. MANAGE YOUR NERVOUS SYMPTOMS.

If speaking before a group makes you nervous, you are not alone. Surveys report that public speaking is the number one fear in the United States, more frightening than snakes, heights, loneliness, and even death. Nervous feelings are the result of adrenaline pumping through your body. Some common manifestations of speech anxiety include butterflies in the stomach, a pounding heart, sweaty palms, a dry mouth, memory loss, shaking limbs, a quivering voice, shortness of breath, and blushing.

The good news is that many of these nervous symptoms aren't visible or audible—which means presenters usually look and sound better than they feel. The audience can't see your pounding heart or sweaty palms. They aren't aware of your dry mouth. They probably won't even notice momentary memory loss. So take comfort in the fact that many of your symptoms can't be detected, and don't berate yourself for feeling nervous. Instead, try to regard the adrenaline rush as a positive element since your delivery might be flat without it. In addition, experiment with the suggestions described in this section until you find the one, or the combination, that helps you manage your nervous symptoms.

1. General techniques

Increase your confidence by analyzing your nervous symptoms and by reminding yourself that you are thoroughly prepared.

Analyze your nervous symptoms.   Identify what symptoms affect you and when they are likely to occur. For instance, you might feel better when you sit down than when you stand. Similarly, you might experience minimal anxiety when the material is familiar but start to panic if the topic is new. Or maybe the size of the group affects you. Some people prefer talking to small groups, while others actually feel more comfortable in front of large audiences.

Once you have thought about when your nervous symptoms are most likely to occur, group them as to whether they are visible or audible to the audience. You may want to focus only on those that are noticeable or you may prefer to begin with the symptoms that bother you the most.

- *Body language:* If your nervous symptoms are related to body language—such as pacing, fidgeting, or darting eye contact—review the material on body position, movement, hand and arm gesturing, eye contact, and facial expression at the beginning of this chapter (pages 112–117) and then try some of the physical relaxation techniques described later in this chapter on pages 130–131.

- *Vocal traits:* If your symptoms relate to vocal traits, review the material about volume, rate, inflection, and filler words on pages 117–120. Then look at the vocal advice on page 131.

Prepare and rehearse.   If you have followed the suggestions we have made so far, you have used an effective process to prepare and rehearse. This knowledge should build your confidence and help calm you down.

- *Be confident because you have used a strategic approach.* If you have "aimed," you have done the necessary strategic work. Your material will be appropriate for the audience, your objective will be clear, and you will have ordered the material so that it will hold the audience's attention and be easy to recall.

- *Benefit from having a clear structure.* If you have a good opening with a preview, then both you and the audience will be very aware of how you plan to structure your talk. If you have organized the body into a small number of sections, you will have no trouble remembering which section comes next. If you have created and rehearsed your backward/forward looking transitions, you won't get stuck wondering how to move to the next part of your talk. And if you have prepared a strong closing, you won't use a dribble ending, such as muttering "well, that's it, so thanks" as you head for your chair.

- *Practice as suggested earlier in this chapter.* Prepare effective notes. You will have them if you need them. Rehearse out loud and on your feet since knowing something and saying it out loud are two entirely different matters. Check your timing so you don't have too much material and figure out what to cut if your presentation starts late. Make sure you know how to integrate your visual aids into the content of your talk and that you have practiced with the actual visuals you plan to use. If possible, do a rehearsal in the room so you can get used to the space and the furniture arrangement, too.

- *Get some feedback.* If possible, videotape a rehearsal so you can hear and see yourself from the audience's perspective. You might also invite someone to attend one of your rehearsals and ask this person to comment on your content and delivery style.

2. Physical techniques

The following set of techniques is based on the assumption, shared by many athletes and performers, that by relaxing yourself physically, you will calm yourself mentally. Experiment with some of these suggestions until you find one that helps you.

Exercise to control the adrenaline.   One way to channel all the nervous energy that sometimes accompanies a presentation is to exercise on the day of your talk. Many people calm down following the physical exertion of calisthenics, jogging, tennis, or other athletic activities.

Try progressive relaxation.   Developed by psychologist Edmund Jacobson, progressive relaxation involves tensing and relaxing a series of muscle groups. To try this technique:

- *Set aside 20 minutes of undisturbed time* in a comfortable, darkened place where you can lie down.
- *Tense and relax each muscle group.* The various groups include: hands, arms, forehead, neck and throat, upper back, lower back, chest, stomach, buttocks, thighs, calves, and feet. To tense a muscle group, clench vigorously for a full five to seven seconds. To relax, release the tension very quickly. You should experience a warm and pleasant sensation after relaxing each muscle group.
- *Repeat the process.* Tense and relax each muscle group, one after the other. Do the entire process at least twice.

Relax specific body parts.   For some people, stage fright manifests itself in certain parts of the body—for example, tense shoulders, quivering arms, or fidgety hands. Here are some exercises to relax specific body parts:

- *Relax your neck and throat.* Gently roll your neck from side to side, front to back, chin to chest, or all the way around.
- *Relax your shoulders.* Raise one or both shoulders as if you were shrugging. Then roll them back, then down, then forward. After several repetitions, rotate in the opposite direction.
- *Relax your arms.* Shake out your arms, first only at the shoulders, then only at the elbow, finally letting your hands flop at the wrist.
- *Relax your hands.* Repeatedly clench and relax your fists. Start with an open hand and close each finger one by one to make a fist. Hold the position; then release.

Breathe deeply. Controlled breathing exercises are an effective way to lower your heart rate and calm down. The out-breath is the calming one; therefore, emphasize it and not the in-breath. Avoid breathing too fast or doing so much deep breathing that you hyperventilate. Try one or both of these techniques:

- *Emphatic out-breathing:* Breathe in normally through your nose. Then, breathe out though your mouth—either with (1) an audible sigh; (2) a series of short, staccato bursts of air; or (3) one long, continuous stream of air, released as slowly as possible.
- *Metered breathing:* Using a count of four, breathe in and out slowly and comfortably—four in and four out, like a metronome. Then, keeping the same measured pace, breathe in to the count of four, hold the breath to the count of four, and breathe out to the count of eight.

Prepare your voice. Some nervous symptoms affect your voice, causing you to feel short of breath or to produce a cracking or quivering sound. Here are some suggestions for keeping your voice in shape:

- *Practice diaphragmatic breathing.* Diaphragmatic breathing reduces strain on your vocal cords, slows your heart rate, and lowers your pitch. But where exactly is your diaphragm? To find it, put your hand on each of the following places: (1) belly (hand over the navel), (2) high chest (hand over the breastbone) and (3) diaphragm (hand on the bottom half of your rib cage). Now that you know where it is, think of your diaphragm as a balloon. Inhale slowly to make the balloon expand. Inflate it fully to reach your sides and back. Release your breath slowly and the balloon should deflate. Practice inflating and deflating the balloon for at least a minute, preferably lying on your back.
- *Rest and wake up your voice.* Try to get enough sleep the night before your talk. Wake up well before your presentation time to provide a natural warm-up period for your voice.
- *Use warmth to soothe your vocal cords.* (1) Take a long, hot shower, allowing the steam to revive a tired or irritated set of vocal cords. (2) Drink warm liquids, such as herbal tea or water with lemon, that will soothe your throat. Although warm liquids with caffeine are fine for your voice, they can increase your heart rate. Avoid warm milk or hot chocolate because dairy products tend to coat your vocal cords, which can cause problems when you present.
- *Do some vocal warm ups.* Try humming. Begin slowly and quietly. Gradually add a full range of pitches. Then, practice making all the vowel sounds—*a, e, i, o, u*—and perhaps finish your warm-up by singing a favorite song.

3. Mental techniques

Some people find that mental relaxation techniques work better for them—that mental relaxation causes physical relaxation.

Try a positive approach.   Base your thinking on Dale Carnegie's argument: "To feel brave, act as if you are brave. To feel confident, act as if you are confident." He suggests that if you "think positive," you can turn your adrenaline rush into positive energy, motivating the butterflies you feel in your stomach to fly in formation and transforming your negative energy into a positive force. To try this approach, act confident and repeat positive words or phrases before you present, such as "poised, positive, and prepared, poised, positive, and prepared."

Assess your style objectively.   If you have seen and heard yourself on videotape, you should be able to describe, rather than judge, your behaviors. Instead of saying "I looked pathetic in that fig leaf position," notice that your hands were clasped in front of you during the opening of your rehearsal. Then, change your thinking, either by refining your delivery behaviors or by accepting your behaviors as part of your style. To stay away from judgmental thinking, try one of the following approaches (1) think rationally, as described below, or (2) create a positive self-image, as explained on the next page.

Think rationally.   Escape the "ABCs of emotional reactions" as described by psychologist Albert Ellis. Move beyond the following ABCs to reach D, where you are able to dispute the emotional trap:

   A: **A**ctivating event (such as a nervous speaking gesture) sparks an irrational . . .

   B: **B**elief system (such as "What a disaster" or "If I don't look perfect, then I'm terrible"), which causes . . .

   C: **C**onsequences (such as speech anxiety or depression) that can be transcended by . . .

   D: **D**isputing the irrational belief system with rational thought (such as "Now that I'm aware of this gesture, I can work to gradually eliminate it" or "I don't demand perfection from other speakers so why do I demand it from myself?").

Create a positive self-image. Some speakers find positive self-pictures work better than motivational words.

- *Visualize yourself as a successful speaker.* Act out the visualization in your head; see the movie of your upcoming talk, including your polished delivery behaviors and the favorable expressions on the faces in the audience. You may even want to hear their applause.
- *Look at a positive image from a video.* Replay a videotape of yourself giving a presentation. Freeze the video at the point where you really like the image, where your delivery style looks natural and confident. Remember that image when it's time for your next presentation.
- *Imagine yourself as the guru.* To remind yourself that you know your subject matter, remember the times that you have impressed others with your knowledge. See yourself answering people's questions and fascinating them with new ideas.

Picture a calm scene. Relax by conjuring up a visual image of a pleasant scene. Learn how to take your mind from an everyday location to the relaxing place you have visualized.

- *Create a positive place.* On each of the several days before your presentation, close your eyes and imagine a beautiful, calm scene, such as the most beautiful beach you have ever visited. Add details to your image: see the various shades of blue, feel the temperature, and smell the air. Concentrate on your image, excluding everything else, and describe how you feel: "I feel warm and relaxed."
- *Juxtapose the stress.* Several days before your presentation, visualize the place where you are going to present. See the room and the audience; feel the stress. Then, distance yourself. Relax by visualizing the positive place you created for yourself.

Connect with the audience. Think of your audience as individuals and not a vast group of unknown faces. Remember that they are real people.

- *Meet them and greet them.* When people arrive, say "hello" and talk to a few of them. These brief greetings may help you relax.
- *"Befriend" the audience.* Even if you can't greet people in the room, try to think of them as individuals. Imagine having conversations with them. You may even want to think of them as potential friends, picturing them in your home, enthusiastically talking with you in a warm and pleasant atmosphere.

4. Last-minute tips

When it's actually time to deliver the presentation, try a few of the following relaxation techniques. Some of them can even be used as you speak.

Manage your physical symptoms.   Obviously, you cannot start doing push-ups or practice humming when you are in the room waiting to present. Fortunately, there are a few subtle techniques you can use at the last minute to relax your body and help your voice:

- *Try isometric exercise.* These quick exercises can be used discretely to steady shaking hands or prevent tapping feet. Isometric exercises involve clenching and then quickly relaxing your muscles. For example, you might put your hands behind your back, tightly clench your fists, and then quickly relax your hands. Or, before you get up to speak, you might press or wiggle your feet against the floor, clench these muscles, and then relax your feet.

- *Take a deep breath.* Inhale slowly and deeply. Exhale completely. Imagine you are breathing in "the good" and out "the bad." A deep breath can slow your heart rate. Also use it to remind yourself that pausing gives you a chance to take in all the air your voice will need to make sound effectively.

- *Sip water.* If you suffer from a dry mouth, drink some water before you go up to present. Have a glass of water available as you present so you can pause, and take a sip, as needed.

Improve your mental state.   Also, at the last minute, you can dispel stage fright by using what psychologists call "internal dialogue," which means, of course, talking to yourself. Here are some of the messages you may want to generate:

- *Give yourself a pep talk.* Act like a coach and deliver motivational messages to yourself, such as "I'm prepared and ready to do a great job. My visual aids are first-rate. I can answer any question that comes my way."

- *Play up the audience's reception.* Look at the audience and find something positive to say about them: "These people are really going to be interested in what I have to say" or "They seem like a very friendly group."

- *Repeat positive phrases.* Develop an internal mantra that can help you overcome your fears, such as "I know my stuff; I know my stuff" or "I'm glad I'm here; I'm glad I'm here."

Relax as you speak. Finally, here are four ways to relax while you are in front of your audience.

- *Speak to the interested listeners.* There are always a few kind souls in the audience who nod, smile, and react favorably. Especially early in the presentation, look at them and not at the people who are reading, starting out the window, or yawning. Seeing the engaged and friendly listeners will increase your confidence and soon you will feel able to look throughout the room.
- *Talk to someone in the back.* To make sure your voice sounds strong and confident, take a deep breath and talk to someone sitting in the back. Try to maintain this audible volume throughout your talk.
- *Know that you probably look and sound better than you feel.* Your nervousness is probably not as apparent to your audience as it is to you. Experiments show that even trained speech instructors do not see all the nervous symptoms speakers think they are exhibiting. Managers and students watching videotapes of their performances regularly say, "Hey, I look better than I thought I would!"
- *Concentrate on the here and now.* Focus on your ideas and your audience. Forget about past regrets and future uncertainties. You have already analyzed what to do—now just do it wholeheartedly.

———————

In closing, we hope we have created an easy-to-follow guide that helps you prepare your presentation from start to finish. Whether you are an experienced presenter or just a beginner, we recommend that you:

- **AIM your efforts,** using the strategic framework described in Part I: analyze the audience, identify your intent, and make the most of the message.
- **Implement your presentation,** using the approach explained in Part II: structure the content, design the visuals, and refine your nonverbal delivery.

In addition to reading these chapters, use the index to find answers to your specific questions and refer to the bibliography to locate useful books, articles, and websites. And remember, you don't need to be perfect, but you do need to AIM.

BIBLIOGRAPHY

This bibliography serves both to acknowledge our sources and to provide readers with references for additional reading. It includes "classics" as well as more recent books, articles, and several useful websites.

BOOKS AND ARTICLES

Adler, N., *International Dimensions of Organizational Behavior,* 5th ed. Australia: South-Western, 2007.

Aristotle, *The Art of Rhetoric.* New York: Penguin Books, 1991.

Baney, J., *Guide to Interpersonal Communication.* Upper Saddle River, NJ: Prentice Hall, 2003.

Bolton, R., *People Skills: How to Assert Yourself, Listen to Others, and Resolve Conflicts.* New York: Simon & Schuster, 1989.

Buzan, T. and B. Buzan, *The Mind Map Book.* London: Pearson Education, 2006.

Cialdini, R., *Influence: Science and Practice,* 4th ed. Boston: Allyn and Bacon, 2001.

——"Harnessing the Science of Persuasion," *Harvard Business Review.* October, 2001, 72–79.

Fischer, M., "Overcoming Message Meltdown" *Strategic Communication Management,* October–November, 1998.

Flower, L. and J. Ackerman, *Problem-Solving Strategies for Writing.* Fort Worth, TX: Harcourt Brace College Publishers, 1998.

French, J. and B. Raven, "The Bases of Social Power" in *Studies in Social Power,* D. Cartwright, (ed.). Ann Arbor: University of Michigan Press, 1959.

Hall, E., *The Hidden Dimension.* New York: Anchor Books, 1992.

Hirsh, S. and J. Kummerow. *Introduction to Type in Organizations.* Palo Alto, CA: CPP, Inc, 1998.

Howell, J., *Tools for Facilitating Meetings.* Seattle: Integrity Publishing, 1995.

Jacobi, J., *How to Say It With Your Voice.* Paramus, NJ: Prentice Hall, 2000.

Jones, G. *How to Lie With Charts.* San Jose, CA: Authors Choice Press, 2001.

Knapp, M. and J. Hall, *Nonverbal Communication in Human Interaction,* 6th ed. Belmont, CA: Thomson Wadsworth, 2005.

Kosslyn S., *Elements of Graph Design.* New York: W.H. Freeman and Company, 1994.

Minto, B., *The Pyramid Principle: Present Your Thinking So Clearly That the Ideas Jump off the Page and into the Reader's Mind,* 3rd ed. London: Minto International, Inc., 2001.

Munter, M., "Cross-Cultural Communication for Managers," *Business Horizons,* May/June 1993.

—— *Guide to Managerial Communication: Effective Writing and Speaking,* 7th ed. Upper Saddle River, NJ: Prentice Hall, 2006.

—— and M. Netzley, *Guide to Meetings.* Upper Saddle River, NJ: Prentice Hall, 2002.

—— and D. Paradi, *Guide to PowerPoint.* Upper Saddle River, NJ: Prentice Hall, 2007.

Murray, D., *Write to Learn,* 7th ed. Fort Worth, TX: Harcourt Brace College, 2004.

Reynolds, S. and D. Valentine, *Guide to Cross-Cultural Communication.* Upper Saddle River, NJ: Prentice Hall, 2004.

Rodenberg, P., *The Right to Speak: Working with the Voice.* New York: Routledge, 1992.

Rose, C., *Accelerated Learning for the 21st Century.* New York: Dell, 1998.

Schenkler, I. and T. Herrling, *Guide to Media Relations.* Upper Saddle River, NJ: Prentice Hall, 2004.

Tannenbaum, R. and W. Schmidt, "How to Choose a Leadership Pattern," *Harvard Business Review,* March–April 1958, 95–101.

Tufte, E., *The Cognitive Style of PowerPoint.* Cheshire, CT: Graphics Press, 2006.

White, J. *Color for Impact: How Color Can Get Your Message Across—or Get in the Way.* Berkeley CA: Strathmoor Press, 1997.

Williams, R. *The Non-Designer's Design Book: Design & Typographic Principles for the Visual Novice,* 3rd ed. Berkeley, CA: Peachpit Press, 2005.

Yates, J. "Persuasion: What the Research Tells Us," Cambridge, MA: Sloan School, Massachusetts Institute of Technology, 1992.

Zelazny, G. *Say It With Charts Complete Toolkit.* New York: McGraw-Hill, 2006.

—— *Say It With Presentations, How to Design and Deliver Successful Business Presentations,* 2nd ed. New York: McGraw-Hill, 2006.

WEBSITES

www.berkeley.edu The Berkeley library system offers a comprehensive Internet tutorial to improve your research skills.

www.sec.gov This site links to the plain language handbook provided by the Security and Exchange commission. You will also find a link at www.plainlanguage.gov.

Index